The
Sunday School
Bible

Red-Letter Edition (God & Jesus Christ)
Based on the King James Version
Jesus's Bloodline Highlighted

God said…in the
Book of Genesis

Prior to 4000 BC–1806 BC

Copyright

This book was written to honor
the LORD (YAHWEH) our GOD (ELOHIM)
and HIS SON JESUS CHRIST (YESHUA)

May the LORD (YAHWEH) give
knowledge, understanding, and wisdom
to all who read this book.

For the LORD [YAHWEH] grants wisdom!
From HIS mouth comes knowledge and understanding.
HE grants a treasure of common sense to the honest.
HE is a shield to those who walk with integrity.

—Proverbs 2:6–7

May the LORD [YAHWEH] bless you and protect you.
May the LORD [YAHWEH] smile on you and be gracious to you.
May the LORD [YAHWEH] show you HIS favor and give you HIS peace.

—Numbers 6:24–26

Contents

Stories

Learning is even easier now through The Sunday School Bible Lessons. View additional Bible stories from the Book of Genesis at www.TheSundaySchoolBible.com

Story
Genealogies in the Book of Genesis
The Story of Creation
The Story of Adam and Eve
The Story of Cain and Abel
The Story of Noah
The Story of the Tower of Babel
The Story of Abraham
The Story of Sodom and Gomorrah
The Story of Isaac
The Story of Jacob
The Story of Joseph

Introduction

Translation Philosophy

There are so many Bible translations worldwide; why would anyone want to read *The Sunday School Bible*?

The Sunday School Bible (*SSB*) is designed specifically for you, the reader. Yes, there are many other Bible translations in the world that you can read and probably have tried reading, but you just might find the *SSB* to be the easiest and most enjoyable. Why is that, you might ask?

There are over one hundred English Bible translations worldwide, each of them focusing on translating the original text into either a formal or functional translation. The list below provides a quick overview of a few well-known Bible translations in formal and functional equivalence while trying to also structure sentences in easy, medium, or difficult reading levels.

- Formal equivalence (word-for-word) translations:

    o King James Version (KJV)
    o New King James Version (NKJV)
    o English Standard Version (ESV)
    o New Revised Standard Version, Updated Edition (NRSVUE)
    o New American Standard Bible (NASB)
    o Christian Standard Bible (CSB)
    o New American Bible Revised Edition (NABRE)

- Functional equivalence (thought-for-thought) translations:

    o New International Version (NIV)
    o New Living Translation (NLT)
    o Common English Bible (CEB)

If you are like me, you may have had no idea there were so many different translations, the difference between formal and functional equivalence, or that reading levels were even a factor in a translation. Knowing now that there are over one hundred different English Bible translations formatted into these different scriptural equivalences as well as easy, medium, and difficult reading levels, it's no wonder we buy so many Bibles trying to find the one that we can read as well as understand.

The *SSB* uses the KJV as the baseline translation. Therefore, the *SSB* does not try to re-translate the original text of the Bible like all other Bible translations. The *SSB* uses the KJV as its baseline translation because it is well-known that many Christians worldwide consider the KJV the most accurate English translation available today. Furthermore, the KJV has been described as one of the most important books in English culture and remains the preferred translation of many Protestant Christians. Many Evangelicals considered the KJV the only "valid" Bible translation. Therefore, many people like me have always had a desire to read the KJV but have found it so difficult to read and understand that we equate it to reading a foreign language. Because of this, the *SSB*'s focus is to transform the KJV style, language, and formatting into modern-day English so that people of all ages can easily read the KJV and easily understand GOD'S WORD speaking to them.

Formatting Philosophy

Reformatting a book like the KJV is no easy task, and I'm sure it will come with a lot of scrutiny. However, spending so many hours meticulously reading each word of each sentence of each chapter to ensure such an important and well-respected manuscript's meaning is not altered but elevated to reach all ages could not have been completed without GOD'S light shining on me. This effort, by no means, could have been my work; the continuous day-to-day drive and focus to produce the *SSB* before the LORD'S return could only have been inspired and guided by GOD.

I reviewed each word and sentence in the KJV hundreds of times to ensure its readability and understandability. In order to do this review, I first transcribed the KJV onto 8.5-inch-by-11-inch paper since this was the normal size paper on which I had always worked. I then double-spaced each sentence to ensure each could be read and understood independently. I discovered that each sentence is profoundly important when read on its own, needless to say when read in context with other phrases, paragraphs, and chapters.

As I read and reread each word and each sentence for reading ease, I also read for understanding. Oftentimes, sentences would be easy to read but

12

didn't make sense, or they made sense but were very difficult to read. Therefore, I researched the areas within each sentence that caused a reading delay or gap in understanding and focused on solving that particular dilemma. I would often have to restructure or reformat a sentence, use a synonym for a word, and research other biblical translations and footnotes to identify other meanings for the same word or sentence. Collectively, this effort surfaced the numerous different translations in other Bible translations and the confusion caused by formal or functional translations and translation efforts that incorporated different reading levels. Overall, the numerous research in other Bible translations related to each KJV word, sentence, and paragraph formed my understanding of what GOD was trying to convey through the KJV. The KJV word or sentence was maintained whenever there were complete differences between other translated texts to that of the KJV. Again, using the KJV text as the baseline and comparing it to other Bible translations only confirmed the power of the KJV. Therefore, maintaining the KJV translation was extremely important. Maintaining this approach helps easily convey the thoughts behind the text to ensure the text is not misleading or confusing to modern readers.

Unique Features

Small capital letters: The *SSB* honors GOD and JESUS CHRIST by highlighting the spelling of names using small capital letters. The main reason for small capitals versus large capitals is that small capitals are easier to read. Large capitals tend to be more difficult for readers and sometimes appear to imply yelling or an elevation in tone. Therefore, the *SSB* maintains lowercase capital letters to ensure reading is fluid while maintaining an elevated level of honor.

Names: The desire to know GOD and research every line of the Bible encouraged many hours of research. Through this research, I discovered that in the scripture, GOD was listed by many names. The more research I conducted, the more important these more specific names for GOD became. Therefore, in order to ensure the reader could feel a connection to GOD, the *SSB* makes a point of specifically identifying the names of GOD throughout the KJV text. For example, in Genesis 1, GOD (ELOHIM) is used. In Genesis 2, LORD (YAHWEH) GOD (ELOHIM) is used. In Genesis 4, LORD (YAHWEH) is used. In Genesis 15, LORD (YAHWEH) GOD (ADONAI) is used. Reading through the Bible is powerful as is, and identifying the different names used in original scripture within the KJV elevates the reader's understanding of GOD and the importance of HIS names in scripture. Therefore, the *SSB* repeatedly conveys through

13

parenthesis the original names used to ensure the reader comprehends the gravity of each sentence by the name used. The *SSB* maintains this method of identification to enhance the presence of GOD in the text, transforming the reading into a personal mentoring by GOD, differentiating the Bible from a normal book.

Red text: The red-letter edition of the Bible began in 1899. The thought behind the red text was to acknowledge JESUS CHRIST'S blood that was shed for our sins or, as JESUS states in Luke 22:20, "This cup is the New Testament in MY blood, which is shed for you." These red-letter editions are extremely valuable to the reader when learning the exact words JESUS spoke. In my research, however, I could not find an equivalent highlight to the words that GOD spoke, which was concerning. I researched extensively and was disappointed to find that few to no Bible translations color-coded the words GOD spoke. The problem with this is that I wanted to know GOD on a personal level and therefore, wanted to know exactly what HE said, to whom HE said it, when HE said it, why HE said it, and how HE said it. However, I could not find a translation that presented the text in this way. Therefore, since I believe in the TRINITY and want to ensure I do not miss an opportunity to honor the LORD (YAHWEH) and my GOD (ELOHIM), I wanted to make sure HIS spoken WORD was highlighted in red text as well. Therefore, the *SSB* highlights in red text the spoken WORDS of both GOD and JESUS CHRIST. I understand that red-letter edition loyalists may find this offensive, but for those who are believers in the TRINITY, I believe this red text format will only honor GOD more. Honoring GOD is the purpose of the *SSB*.

Limited page count: The *SSB* focuses on the reader and therefore, wants to ensure that the size of just looking at a book is not too intimidating. Therefore, the *SSB* uses limited page counts to ensure each book is inviting to pick up and read. Furthermore, the reader feels accomplished and confident in completing each book, motivating them to start reading the next book of the Bible. Again, everything about the *SSB* focuses on the reader.

The 11-point font on 8.5-inch-by-11-inch paper: The *SSB* is formatted using this standard-sized font on standard-sized paper because it is the standard size we have used since we were young. Unlike the normal 7- or 8-point font used in a two-column standard Bible, the SSB uses the normal 11-point font on an 8.5-inch-by-11-inch size piece of paper. The standard font size and larger paper size allow for much easier reading. The thicker paper also facilitates the use of highlighters and pins without concern for ink bleeding onto the next page. Additionally, if you are like me, you have torn your fair share of Bible pages and now have a Bible with many taped pages. Those days are gone, thankfully, with the *SSB*.

Contents section: Everyone understands that the contents are valuable areas for identifying chapters of lengthy books. However, the *SSB* uses the contents as a learning tool for the reader. Not only does the *SSB* use chapter references, but it also uses topical section references. To elevate learning even more, the *SSB* includes story sections. Bible stories will often start in the middle of a chapter and end in the middle of another chapter. Therefore, only using chapters and topics is not good enough for the *SSB*. The *SSB* incorporates into the contents where stories begin, even if the beginning of a story is in the middle of a chapter. For example, the story of Cain and Abel, the story of Noah, and the story of Abraham all start at the beginning of a chapter. However, the story of Jacob and Esau starts in the middle of Genesis 25, specifically Genesis 25:21. Therefore, to ensure readers can easily find stories like this, which start in the middle of a chapter, the *SSB* adds this element to its contents. Sunday school teachers and Bible study participants will love this feature.

Double-space: The *SSB* uses double space between sentences to help the reader focus on one sentence at a time. This allows the reader to focus on the importance of understanding what each sentence is saying and the ability to write notes between sentences. Underlining, circling, and highlighting words and phrases is now as easy as it was with your high school or college textbooks—maybe even easier than that.

Quotes: The *SSB* separates all quotable text and defines who is speaking and to whom they are speaking. This format change makes reading the Bible as easy as reading a movie script. Normal Bible translations lack clarity in this area. Often sentences use pronouns (he, him) to convey the participants in the conversation. However, this quickly becomes confusing without the appropriate individual names. To ensure no confusion with who is speaking and to whom they are speaking, the *SSB* replaces the pronouns with the individual's name. Utilizing this format ensures clarity and understanding while also enhancing the fluid reading of each sentence. For example, unlike the normal Bible text where you may see something like "He said to him," the *SSB* clarifies this by replacing it with something like "Joseph said to Jacob." This minor but powerful difference keeps the reader engaged in what is happening in the story without stopping their reading pace to clarify who said what to whom. Fluid reading is a key part of the *SSB*.

Lists: When reading through the normal Bible, especially the KJV, you will encounter many commas and semicolons throughout each sentence. Many Bible versions have modified these sentences into their own modern English narrative. However, the *SSB* tries to keep the KJV sentence structure as much as possible to maintain the power of its narrative. Therefore, the *SSB* takes each element listed between these commas and semicolons and separates them into bulleted lists. These lists help readers categorize each element discussed while also helping them maintain a method to categorize the elements. Ultimately, readers flow easily through these lists instead of getting lost in lengthy sentences. Helping readers with an outline format increases reading pace and learning.

Genealogy: Genealogies in the Bible are often overlooked or just plain too confusing to comprehend. Not only are the names difficult to say but many names are repeated. This challenge is compounded because of the two-column format and small text. Even the most confident Bible-reading Christians admit to passing over genealogies because reading them is so complicated. Therefore, the *SSB* has solved this problem. Understanding that readers learn in different ways and learn best when multiple presentation methods are used, the *SSB* not only lists genealogies in a text format that is easy to understand and comprehend but adds genealogy charts after each text section that restates, graphically, what was just read. This method ensures that the reader does not get lost in the translation but learns the genealogy so that the genealogy can help them better understand the Bible. Unbeknownst to many people, genealogies in the Bible are very important, and most of those listed in these genealogies are referenced in future chapters or books of the Bible.

Purple text: The purple bold text is used to highlight JESUS'S bloodline. When reading the Bible, it is important to understand who GOD chose for this critical lineage. The *SSB* adds this purple highlighted feature to ensure the reader gains further knowledge and understanding of GOD'S WORD as they read. Enhancing the reader's knowledge, understanding, and wisdom as they read is what the *SSB* focuses on.

The same names: The fact that there are many people referenced in the Bible with the same name shouldn't be a surprise to anyone. Similar to today, where we have so many people named Joseph, Tom, Bill, etc., the Bible is no different. However, reading the Bible and seeing the same name for different people forces us to stop and try to identify which individual the Bible is talking about. This investigation causes our reading pace to slow or stop while we confirm which person we are reading about. The *SSB* understands this and has fixed that problem by numbering each person with the same name. For example, Genesis refers to two Enochs, one in Genesis 4:17, which refers to Cain's son, and one in Genesis 5:18–24, which refers to the Enoch whom GOD took. To ensure the reader easily differentiates between these two Enochs while they are reading, the *SSB* clarifies the second Enoch as **Enoch[2]**. When additional individuals are mentioned with the same name, the *SSB* adds [3], [4], and so on to the end of their name. In using this format, the reader's pace does not slow down because they categorically know which individual they are reading about. Additionally, these names are listed in this manner in each genealogy chart to provide a visual learning aid to the reader.

Note brackets: Although footnotes are used in most texts, the *SSB* tries to ensure readers do not have to stop and search for a reference to the sentence they are reading. Therefore, periodically, when a note is needed to clarify a sentence, the *SSB* adds a bracketed note to ensure the reader continues their pace and momentum. An example of an *SSB* note bracket is in Genesis 6:4, where the KJV states, "There were giants on the earth in those days and after." The *SSB* clarifies this to the reader to facilitate their knowledge before reading further by adding a note like the following:

> [Note: The Bible associates the following names and/or tribes to giants: Nephilim, Rephaim, Emim, Zamzummim, the Anakim tribe, and the Amorite tribe.]

By adding this note to the text, the reader now understands that when they read about these additional tribes, they can associate them with giants.

Weights and measures: The *SSB* replaces all weights, measurements, and money with the US customary system of measurement to make reading easy. The reader no longer has to stop reading to look at footnotes for the modern equivalent of cubits, shekels, omers, and the like.

For example, in Genesis 6:15, the KJV states that **Noah's** Ark shall be

- 300 cubits,
- the breadth of it 50 cubits, and
- the height of it 30 cubits.

Reading this for understanding forces the reader to research the size of a cubit, thereby interrupting their reading pace. The *SSB* corrects this dilemma by replacing cubits with the US customary system of measurement:

- four hundred and fifty feet long,
- seventy-five feet wide, and
- forty-five feet high.

Concordance-like index: The *SSB* uses a concordance-like index to make it easy for the reader to research and find names, places, verbs, and GOD'S WORD. Most, if not all, Bibles have limited words in their index. This makes it difficult for readers to quickly search for keywords that they want to find and read about. Therefore, the *SSB* has added to its index key statements that GOD made, names, locations, and numerous other words. This concordance-like index adds a dynamic not found in most Bibles. Allowing readers to quickly look up keywords in the Bible is critical to the learning process and enhances understanding of what GOD is telling us.

* Features marked with an * are not available in black and white versions.

God said…in the Book of Genesis

Chapter 1
Prior to 4000 BC

The Beginning

¹ In the beginning, GOD (ELOHIM) created the heaven and the earth.

² And the earth was without form and void.

Darkness was upon the face of the deep waters.

The SPIRIT OF GOD (RUACH ELOHIM) moved upon the face of the waters.

First Day—Light, Day, and Night

³ GOD (ELOHIM) said,

- "Let there be light!"

And there was light.

⁴ GOD (ELOHIM) saw that the light was good.

Then GOD (ELOHIM) divided the light from the darkness.

⁵ GOD (ELOHIM) called the light day.

GOD (ELOHIM) called the darkness night.

And the evening and the morning were the first day.

Second Day—Heaven

⁶ GOD (ELOHIM) said,

- "Let there be a firmament in the middle of the waters.

- Let the firmament divide the waters from the waters."

⁷ GOD (ELOHIM) made the firmament.

GOD (ELOHIM) divided the waters under the firmament from the waters above the firmament.

And it was so.

[8] GOD (ELOHIM) called the firmament heaven.

And the evening and the morning were the second day.

Third Day—Earth, Sea, and Vegetation

[9] GOD (ELOHIM) said,

- "Let the waters under the heaven be gathered together in one place.

- Let the dry land appear."

And it was so.

[10] GOD (ELOHIM) called the dry land earth.

GOD (ELOHIM) called the gathering together of the waters seas.

And GOD (ELOHIM) saw that it was good.

[11] GOD (ELOHIM) said,

- "Let the earth bring forth the following vegetation upon the earth:
  - grass;
  - herb-yielding seed; and
  - the fruit tree,
  - yielding fruit after his own kind,
  - whose seed is in itself."

And it was so.

[12] And then the earth brought forth the following vegetation upon the earth:
- grass;
- herb-yielding seed after his kind; and
- the tree-yielding fruit,

- whose seed was in itself,
- after his kind.

And GOD (ELOHIM) saw that it was good.

¹³ And the evening and the morning were the third day.

Fourth Day—Sun, Moon, and Stars

¹⁴ GOD (ELOHIM) said,

- "Let there be lights in the firmament of the heaven to divide the day from the night.

- Let the lights in the firmament be used for the following reasons:
  - signs,
  - seasons,
  - days, and
  - years.

- ¹⁵ And let the lights in the firmament of the heaven give light upon the earth."

And it was so.

¹⁶ Then GOD (ELOHIM) made two great lights:
- the greater light to rule the day (the sun) and
- the lesser light to rule the night (the moon).

And GOD (ELOHIM) also made the stars.

¹⁷ GOD (ELOHIM) set the lights in the firmament of heaven for the following reasons:
- to give light upon the earth,
- ¹⁸ to rule over the day,
- to rule over the night, and
- to divide the light from the darkness.

And GOD (ELOHIM) saw that it was good.

¹⁹ And the evening and the morning were the fourth day.

Fifth Day—Fish and Birds

[20] GOD (ELOHIM) said,

- "Let the waters bring forth abundantly the following animals:
  - the moving creatures that have life and
  - the fowl that may fly above the earth in the open firmament of heaven."

[21] Then GOD (ELOHIM) created
- great whales,
- every living creature that moves, which the waters brought forth abundantly after their kind, and
- every winged fowl after his kind.

And GOD (ELOHIM) saw that it was good.

[22] Then GOD (ELOHIM) blessed them, saying,

- "Be fruitful and multiply and
  - fill the waters in the seas and
  - let the fowl multiply on the earth."

[23] And the evening and the morning were the fifth day.

Sixth Day—Animals, Male and Female

[24] GOD (ELOHIM) said,

- "Let the earth bring forth the following living creatures after his kind:
  - cattle,
  - everything that crawls along the ground, and
  - beasts of the earth after his kind."

And it was so.

[25] Then GOD (ELOHIM) made the beasts of the earth after his kind:
- the cattle after their kind and
- everything that creeps upon the earth after his kind.

And GOD (ELOHIM) saw that it was good.

GOD Made Humans
23

[26] GOD (ELOHIM) said,

- "Let US make humans in OUR image, after OUR likeness.

[Note: The KJV and many other English Bible translations use the word "man" in verses such as Genesis 1:26. The original Hebrew Bible used the Hebrew word "אָדָ֜ם" meaning "adam" in Genesis 4:11 and not the Hebrew word for a male man. Furthermore, Genesis 1:27 and Genesis 5:2 confirm the meaning of the word "אָדָ֜ם" or "adam" by referring to both males and females. Therefore, based on Genesis 1:27-26 and Genesis 5:2, the SSB will replace the KJV word "man" with the word "human" wherever the Hebrew text uses the word "אָדָ֜ם" (adam). Using the word "human" or lowercase "adam" instead of "man" in these verses will ensure the reader understands that GOD was referring to all people, not just men.]

- Let humans have dominion over
    o the fish of the sea,
    o the fowl of the air,
    o the cattle,
    o all the earth, and
    o every creeping thing that creeps upon the earth."

[27] So GOD (ELOHIM) created humans in HIS OWN image, in the image of GOD (ELOHIM).

GOD Created Male and Female

GOD (ELOHIM) created male and female.

[28] GOD (ELOHIM) blessed them and said to them,

- "Be fruitful and multiply.

- Replenish the earth and subdue it.

- Have dominion over
    o the fish of the sea,
    o the fowl of the air, and
    o every living thing that moves upon the earth.

- [29] Behold, I have given you the following food for meat:

24

- o every herb bearing seed that is upon the face of all the earth and
- o every tree, in which is the fruit of a tree yielding seed.

- • ³⁰ And to the following animals, I have given every green herb for meat:
  - o every beast of the earth,
  - o every fowl of the air, and
  - o everything that creeps upon the earth wherein there is life."

And it was so.

³¹ And GOD (ELOHIM) saw everything HE had made, and behold, it was very good.

And the evening and the morning were the sixth day.

Chapter 2
Prior to 4000 BC

Seventh Day—GOD Declares the Seventh Day Holy

[1] The heavens and the earth were finished, and all the host of them.

[2] On the seventh day, GOD (ELOHIM) ended HIS work, which HE had made, and HE rested.

[3] GOD (ELOHIM) blessed the seventh day and sanctified it (made it holy).

GOD (ELOHIM) made the seventh day holy because HE had rested on the seventh day from all HIS work, which HE created and made.

Generations of the Heavens and the Earth

[4] These are the generations of the heavens and of the earth when they were created in the day that the LORD GOD (YAHWEH ELOHIM) made
- the earth,
- the heavens,
- [5] every plant of the field before it was in the earth, and
- every herb of the field before it grew.

At this time, the LORD GOD (YAHWEH ELOHIM) had not caused it to rain upon the earth.

Also, there was not a man to till the ground.

[6] But there went up a mist from the earth that watered the whole face of the ground.

[7] The LORD GOD (YAHWEH ELOHIM) formed a human from the dust of the ground.

The LORD GOD (YAHWEH ELOHIM) breathed the breath of life into the human's nostrils, and the human/adam (Adam) became a living soul (adam/Adam means ground or earth).

Garden of Eden

[8] The LORD GOD (YAHWEH ELOHIM) planted a garden eastward in Eden (Garden of Eden).

There HE put the human (Adam) whom HE had formed.

[9] The LORD GOD (YAHWEH ELOHIM) made every tree grow out of the ground, which is pleasant to look at and good for food.

In the middle of the Garden of Eden were also the following two trees:
- the tree of life and
- the tree of knowledge of good and evil.

[10] A river went out of Eden to water the Garden of Eden.

From there, the river was divided into four heads:
- Pison River,
- Gihon River,
- Hiddekel River, and
- Euphrates River.

[11] Pison is the name of the first river.

- This river encompassed the whole land of Havilah, where there was gold.

- [12] The gold of that land was good and contained
  o bdellium and
  o onyx stone.

[13] Gihon is the name of the second river.

- This river encompassed the whole land of Ethiopia.

[14] Hiddekel is the name of the third river.

- This river flowed toward the east of Assyria.

Euphrates is the name of the fourth river.

[15] The LORD GOD (YAHWEH ELOHIM) took the man (Adam) and put him in the Garden of Eden to dress it and to keep it.

The Tree of Knowledge of Good and Evil

[16] The LORD GOD (YAHWEH ELOHIM) commanded the man (**Adam**), saying,

- "You may eat freely from every tree in the garden of Eden.

- [17] But you must not eat from the tree of knowledge of good and evil.

- For in the day you eat from it, you will surely die."

GOD Made Woman (**Eve**)

[18] Then the LORD GOD (YAHWEH ELOHIM) said,

- "It is not good for the man to be alone.

- I will make him a helper who is right for him."

[19] And out of the ground, the LORD GOD (YAHWEH ELOHIM) formed the following animals:
- every beast of the field and
- every fowl of the air.

The LORD GOD (YAHWEH ELOHIM) brought them to **Adam** to see what he would call them.

Whatsoever **Adam** called every living creature, that was its name.

[20] **Adam** gave names to all of the following animals:
- cattle,
- fowl of the air, and
- every beast of the field.

But for the human (**Adam**), a helper was still not found for him.

[21] Then the LORD GOD (YAHWEH ELOHIM) caused a deep sleep to fall upon **Adam**, and **Adam** slept.

The LORD GOD (YAHWEH ELOHIM) took one of **Adam's** ribs and then closed the flesh.

²² The LORD GOD (YAHWEH ELOHIM) made a woman from the rib, which HE had taken from the man, and brought her to the man (Adam).

Adam said,

- ²³ "This is now bone of my bones, flesh of my flesh.

- She will be called a woman because she was taken out of man."

²⁴ Therefore, when a man leaves his father and mother, he will cleave to his wife, and they will be one flesh.

²⁵ And they were both naked, the man (Adam) and his wife (Eve), and were not ashamed.

Chapter 3
Prior to 4000 BC

The Serpent (a.k.a. Satan—the Devil)

¹ The serpent (also known as Satan/the devil) was more subtle than any beast of the field that the LORD GOD (YAHWEH ELOHIM) had made.

The serpent said to the woman (**Eve**),

- "Did GOD [ELOHIM] say that you must not eat from every tree of the Garden of Eden?"

² The woman (**Eve**) said to the serpent,

- "We may eat the fruit from the trees in the Garden of Eden.

- ³ But, the fruit from the tree which is in the middle of the Garden of Eden, GOD [ELOHIM] said,

  o 'You must not eat of it or touch it, or else you will die.'"

⁴ The serpent said to the woman (**Eve**),

- "You will not die from eating the fruit.

- ⁵ GOD [ELOHIM] knows that the moment you eat the fruit, your eyes will be opened, and you will be like GOD [ELOHIM], knowing good and evil."

The First Sin

⁶ When the woman (**Eve**) saw that the tree was good for food, that it was pleasant to the eyes, and was a tree to be desired because it could make one wise, the woman (**Eve**)
  o took the fruit from the tree;
  o ate the fruit;
  o gave the fruit to her husband, **Adam**, who was with her; and
  o **Adam** ate it.

7 And the eyes of them both were opened, and they knew they were naked.

They sewed fig leaves together and made aprons to cover themselves.

8 Then, they heard the voice of the LORD GOD (YAHWEH ELOHIM) walking in the Garden of Eden in the cool part of the day.

Adam and his wife (Eve) hid themselves from the presence of the LORD GOD (YAHWEH ELOHIM) amongst the trees of the Garden of Eden.

9 The LORD GOD (YAHWEH ELOHIM) called to Adam, saying,

- "Where are you?"

10 Adam said to the LORD GOD (YAHWEH ELOHIM),

- "I heard YOUR voice in the Garden of Eden, and I was afraid because I was naked.

- Therefore, I hid myself."

11 The LORD GOD (YAHWEH ELOHIM) said to Adam,

- "Who told you that you were naked?

- Have you eaten from the tree of knowledge of good and evil, from which I commanded you not to eat?"

12 Adam said to the LORD GOD (YAHWEH ELOHIM),

- "The woman [Eve] whom YOU gave to me, she gave me fruit from the tree, and I ate it."

13 The LORD GOD (YAHWEH ELOHIM) said to the woman (Eve),

- "What is this that you have done?"

The woman (Eve) said to the LORD GOD (YAHWEH ELOHIM),

- "The serpent deceived me, and I ate it."

GOD Curses the Serpent

31

¹⁴ The LORD GOD (YAHWEH ELOHIM) said to the serpent,

- "Because you have done this, you are cursed
    - above all cattle and
    - above every beast of the field.

- Upon your belly, you will crawl.

- You will eat dust all the days of your life.

- ¹⁵ I will put hostility between
    - you and the woman [**Eve**] and
    - between your seed [descendants] and her seed [descendants].

- It will bruise your head, and you will bruise his heel."

GOD Curses Woman

¹⁶ The LORD GOD (YAHWEH ELOHIM) said to the woman (**Eve**),

- "I will greatly multiply your sorrow and your conception.

- You will bring forth children in sorrow.

- Your desire will be for your husband.

- Your husband will rule over you."

GOD Curses Adam

¹⁷ The LORD GOD (YAHWEH ELOHIM) said to **Adam**,

- "Because you have listened to the voice of your wife and have eaten from the tree from which I commanded you not to, saying,

    - 'You must not eat of it.'

- Cursed is the ground for your sake.

- In sorrow, you will eat from the ground all the days of your life.

- [18] The ground will only grow thorns and thistles for you.

- You will eat the herb of the field.

- [19] In the sweat of your face [exhaustion from harvesting], you will eat bread until you return to the ground because out of the ground you were taken.

- From dust you were made, and into dust, you will return."

[20] **Adam** called his wife's name **Eve** (**Eve** means to live or life) because she was the mother of all living things.

[21] The LORD GOD (YAHWEH ELOHIM) made coats of skins for **Adam** and **Eve** and clothed them.

[22] And the LORD GOD (YAHWEH ELOHIM) said,

- "Behold, the human has become as one of US, to know good and evil.

- What if the human puts forth his hand, takes fruit from the tree of life, eats it, and lives forever?"

[23] Therefore, the LORD GOD (YAHWEH ELOHIM) sent the man (**Adam**) away from the Garden of Eden to the ground from which he was taken.

[24] So after the LORD GOD (YAHWEH ELOHIM) sent them away.

The LORD GOD (YAHWEH ELOHIM) placed cherubim (divine creatures) and a flaming sword at the east of the Garden of Eden.

The flaming sword turned in all directions to guard the way to the tree of life.

Chapter 4
Prior to 3000 BC

Cain and Abel

[1] **Adam** had intercourse with his wife **Eve**, and she conceived and gave birth to Cain.

Eve said to herself,

- "I have received a man from the LORD [YAHWEH]."

[2] And **Eve** again gave birth, this time to Cain's brother, Abel:
- Cain was a tiller of the ground.
- Abel was a keeper of sheep.

[3] In the process of time, it came to pass that Cain and Abel brought the following offerings to the LORD (YAHWEH):
- Cain brought fruit from the ground.
- [4] Abel brought the firstborn of his flock and of its fat.

The LORD (YAHWEH) respected Abel and his offering, [5] but HE did not respect Cain or his offering.

Cain was very angry, and he displayed disappointment on his face.

[6] The LORD (YAHWEH) said to Cain,

- "Why are you angry?

- Why has your demeanor changed?

- [7] If you do well, you will be accepteddo.

- If you do not do well, sin will lie at the door, and you will be his [sin's] desire.

- So you must rule over him [sin]."

Cain Kills Abel

[8] Cain talked with Abel, his brother.

And it came to pass when they were in the field, Cain rose up against Abel, his brother, and killed him.

[9] The LORD (YAHWEH) said to Cain,

- "Where is your brother Abel?"

Cain said to the LORD (YAHWEH),

- "I don't know: Am I my brother's keeper?"

[10] The LORD (YAHWEH) said to Cain,

- "What have you done?

- The voice of your brother's blood cries out to ME from the ground.

- [11] Now you are cursed from the earth, which has opened her mouth to receive your brother's blood from your hand.

- [12] When you till the ground, it will no longer produce crops for you.

- You will be a homeless wanderer on the earth."

[13] Cain said to the LORD (YAHWEH),

- "My punishment is greater than I can endure.

- [14] Today, YOU have driven me from the face of the earth.

- I will hide myself from YOUR face.

- I will be a fugitive and a vagabond on the earth, and it will come to pass that anyone who finds me will kill me."

[15] The LORD (YAHWEH) said to Cain,

- "Whosoever kills Cain, vengeance will be taken on him

sevenfold."

Then the LORD (YAHWEH) set a mark on Cain, to warn those who may want to kill him.

[16] Cain left the presence of the LORD (YAHWEH) and lived in the land of Nod, east of Eden.

Cain's Descendants

[17] Later, Cain had intercourse with his wife (no name given).

Cain's wife conceived and gave birth to a son named Enoch.

[Note: This is not the same Enoch as Enoch[2] whom GOD took in Genesis 5:18–24.]

Cain built a city named after his son: Enoch City.

[18] Enoch became the father of
- Irad.

Irad became the father of
- Mehujael.

Mehujael became the father of
- Methushael.

Methushael became the father of
- Lamech.

Lamech's Children

[19] Lamech married the following two wives:
- Adah and
- Zillah.

[20] Adah gave birth to
- Jabal.

Jabal was the father of those who lived in tents and had cattle.

[21] His brother's name was

- Jubal.

Jubal was the father of all who handled the harp and organ.

²² Zillah also gave birth to
- Tubalcain (also spelled Tubal-Cain in other texts).

Tubalcain was an instructor of every artificer (craftsman) in brass and iron.

Tubalcain's sister was
- Naamah.

²³ Lamech said to his wives Adah and Zillah,

- "Hear my voice, you wives of Lamech, listen to my speech.

- I have killed a man for wounding me and a young man for hurting me.

- ²⁴ If Cain can be avenged sevenfold, truly I can be avenged seventy-seven times."

Seth is Born

²⁵ Adam had intercourse with Eve again.

Eve gave birth to a son and called his name
- Seth.

Eve said to herself,

- "GOD (ELOHIM) has given me another seed [child] instead of Abel, whom Cain killed."

²⁶ A son was also born to Seth; Adam named him
- Enos (also spelled Enosh in other texts).

At that time, men began to call on the name of the LORD (YAHWEH).

Chapter 6
Prior to 2500 BC

120-Year-Old Limit

[1] And it came to pass that when men began to multiply on the face of the earth and daughters were born to them, [2] the sons of GOD (ELOHIM) (also known in the Bible as giants called Nephilim) saw that daughters of men were beautiful, and they took all they wanted for wives.

[3] The LORD (YAHWEH) said,

- "MY SPIRIT will not always strive with man because man is flesh.

- Therefore, man's days will only be one hundred and twenty years."

Giants

[4] There were giants on the earth in those days and after.

[Note: The Bible associates the following names and/or tribes to giants: Nephilim, Rephaim, Emim, Zamzummim, and the Anakim tribe.]

When the sons of GOD (ELOHIM) had intercourse with the daughters of men and the women gave birth to children, the children became mighty men, men of renown.

[5] GOD (ELOHIM) saw that the wickedness of man was great on the earth.

GOD (ELOHIM) saw that every imagination of thought within a man's heart was only evil continually.

[6] The LORD (YAHWEH) was sorry that HE had made man on the earth.

It grieved the LORD (YAHWEH) in HIS heart.

[7] The LORD (YAHWEH) said,

- "I will destroy man (every living thing) from the face of the

earth, whom I created, both
  - o   man,
  - o   beast,
  - o   the creeping things, and
  - o   the fowls of the air.

- It repents ME that I made them."

⁸ But **Noah** found grace in the eyes of the LORD (YAHWEH).

Noah's Sons

⁹ These are the generations of **Noah**.

Noah was a just man and perfect in his generation.

Noah walked with GOD (ELOHIM).

¹⁰ **Noah** had the following three sons:
- **Shem**,
- Ham, and
- Japheth.

¹¹ At this time, the earth was corrupt before GOD (ELOHIM), and the earth was filled with violence.

¹² GOD (ELOHIM) looked upon the earth and saw that it was corrupt because all the flesh had corrupted itself upon the earth.

Noah Builds an Ark

¹³ GOD (ELOHIM) said to **Noah**,

- "The end of all flesh has come before ME.

- The earth is filled with violence through them.

- I will destroy them with the earth.

- ¹⁴ Make yourself an ark of cypress [gopher] wood.

- You will make rooms in the ark.

- You will waterproof the ark inside and outside with tar [pitch].

- [15] You will construct the ark using the following dimensions:
  - four hundred and fifty feet long,
  - seventy-five feet wide, and
  - forty-five feet high.

- [16] You will put a window on the ark and place it eighteen inches below the roof.

- You will place the ark's door on the side of the ark.

- You will build three floors inside the ark:
  - a lower deck,
  - a second story, and
  - a third story.

- [17] I, even I, am bringing a flood of waters upon the earth to destroy all flesh, wherein is the breath of life, from under heaven.

- Everything that is on the earth will die.

- [18] But I will establish MY covenant with you.

- You will come into the ark:
  - you,
  - your sons,
  - your wife, and
  - your sons' wives.

- [19] You will bring into the ark every living thing of all flesh, two of every sort, to keep them alive with you; they will be male and female.

- [20] You will take two of every sort of animal with you so you can keep them alive:
  - the fowls after their kind,
  - the cattle after their kind, and
  - every creeping thing of the earth after his kind.

40

- ²¹ For yourselves, gather all food that can be eaten; it will be food for you and for them."

²² **Noah** did all that GOD (ELOHIM) commanded him to do.

Chapter 7
Prior to 2500 BC

The Flood Starts

¹ The LORD (YAHWEH) said to **Noah**,

- "Come you and all your house into the ark.

- I have seen your righteousness before ME in this generation.

- ² You must take seven pairs of every clean beast with you, male and his female.

- You must take one pair of each unclean beast with you, male and his female.

- ³ You must take seven pairs of every fowl of the air with you, male and the female.

- This way, you will keep their seed alive on the face of all the earth.

- ⁴ In seven days, I will cause it to rain on the earth for forty days and forty nights.

- I will destroy every living substance from off the face of the earth that I have made."

⁵ **Noah** did according to all the LORD (YAHWEH) commanded him.

⁶ **Noah** was six hundred years old when the flood of waters was upon the earth.

⁷ **Noah** went into the ark, because of the flood waters, with the following:
- his sons,
- his wife,
- his sons' wives,
- ⁸ the clean beasts,
- the unclean beasts,

- the fowls, and
- everything that creeps upon the earth.

⁹ All of them went into the ark two by two, the male and the female, as GOD (ELOHIM) had commanded **Noah**.

¹⁰ And it came to pass, after seven days, the waters of the flood were upon the earth.

¹¹ In the six hundredth year of **Noah's** life, in the second month, the seventeenth day of the month, on the same day, the following occurred
- All the underground fountains erupted and
- The windows of heaven opened.

¹² The rain was upon the earth for forty days and forty nights.

¹³ On the same day, the following people and animals entered the ark:
- **Noah**,
- **Shem**,
- Ham,
- Japheth,
- **Noah's** wife,
- **Noah's** three daughters-in-law,
- ¹⁴ every beast after his kind,
- all the cattle after their kind,
- every creeping thing that creeps upon the earth after his kind,
- every fowl after his kind, and
- every bird of every sort.

¹⁵ They went into the ark with **Noah**, two by two of all flesh, wherein is the breath of life.

¹⁶ And those who went into the ark, entered by male and female of all flesh, as GOD (ELOHIM) had commanded **Noah**.

And the LORD (YAHWEH) shut him in (closed the door behind **Noah**).

¹⁷ It flooded on earth for forty days.

The waters increased, the ark raised up, and the ark was lifted up above the earth.

¹⁸ The waters prevailed and increased greatly upon the earth.

The ark floated upon the face of the waters.

¹⁹ The waters prevailed exceedingly upon the earth.

All the high hills under all of heaven were covered with water.

²⁰ The waters rose twenty-two feet above the highest mountains.

²¹ All flesh that moved upon the earth died
- fowl,
- cattle,
- beast,
- every creeping thing that creeps upon the earth, and
- every human.

²² All in whose nostrils was the breath of life, of all that was in the dry land, died.

²³ Every living substance was destroyed that was upon the face of the ground:
- human,
- cattle,
- creeping things, and
- the fowl of the heaven.

They were all destroyed from the earth.

Only **Noah** and those who were with him in the ark remained alive.

²⁴ The waters remained on earth for one hundred and fifty days.

Chapter 8
Prior to 2500 BC

The Ground Dries

¹ GOD (ELOHIM) remembered Noah, every living thing, and all the cattle with Noah in the ark.

GOD (ELOHIM) made a wind pass over the earth, and the waters eased.

² The fountains of the deep and the windows of heaven stopped.

The rain from heaven was restrained.

³ The waters returned from being on the earth continually.

The waters stopped after one hundred fifty days (five months from when the flood first started).

⁴ The ark rested upon the Ararat mountains in the seventh month, on the seventeenth day of the month.

⁵ The waters decreased continually until the tenth month.

⁶ It came to pass that after forty days, Noah opened the window of the ark he had made.

⁷ Noah sent forth a raven, which flew back and forth until the waters were dried up from off the earth.

⁸ Noah also sent forth a dove to see if the waters had completely subsided from the face of the ground.

⁹ But the dove found no rest for the sole of her foot, so the dove returned to Noah and into the ark.

The waters were still on the face of the whole earth.

Then Noah put forth his hand and took the dove, pulling the dove back to himself and into the ark.

¹⁰ After another seven days, **Noah** again sent forth the dove out of the ark.

¹¹ In the evening, the dove returned to him with a freshly plucked olive leaf in her mouth.

So **Noah** knew that the waters had subsided from the earth.

¹² **Noah** stayed in the ark for another seven days.

Then, **Noah** rereleased the dove.

This time the dove never returned.

¹³ And it came to pass, in the six hundred and first year, in the first month, on the first day of the month, the waters were dried up from off the earth.

Noah removed the ark's covering and saw that the face of the ground was dry.

¹⁴ In the second month, on the twenty-seventh day of the month, the earth was dry.

The Ground Dries—Noah Departs the Ark

¹⁵ GOD (ELOHIM) said to **Noah**,

- ¹⁶ "Depart the ark
  - you,
  - your wife,
  - your sons, and
  - your daughters-in-law.

- ¹⁷ Take every living thing that is with you, of all flesh:
  - fowl,
  - cattle, and
  - every creeping thing that creeps upon the earth.

- Do this so they may
  - breed abundantly in the earth,
  - be fruitful, and
  - multiply upon the earth."

¹⁸ **Noah** departed the ark with
- his sons,
- his wife,
- his daughters-in-law,
- ¹⁹ every beast,
- every creeping thing,
- every fowl, and
- whatsoever crept on the earth after their kind went forth out of the ark.

²⁰ **Noah** built an altar to the LORD (YAHWEH).

Noah offered burnt offerings on the altar of every type of
- clean beast and
- clean fowl.

²¹ The LORD (YAHWEH) smelled a sweet aroma.

The LORD (YAHWEH) said in HIS heart,

- "I will not again curse the ground anymore for man's sake because the imagination of man's heart is evil from his youth.

- I will never again strike every living thing as I have done.

- ²² While the earth remains, the following will not cease:
  - seed time and harvest,
  - cold and heat,
  - summer and winter, and
  - day and night."

Chapter 9
Prior to 2500 BC

GOD Blesses Noah

[1] GOD (ELOHIM) blessed **Noah** and his sons and said to them,

- "Be fruitful, multiply, and replenish the earth.

- [2] The fear of you and the dread of you will be upon
    - every beast on earth,
    - every fowl of the air,
    - all that moves upon the earth, and
    - all the fish in the sea.

- They are delivered into your hand.

- [3] Every moving thing that lives will be meat for you, just as I have given you all green herbs.

- [4] But you must not eat flesh with life still in it, which is the blood within it.

- [5] I will account for the blood of your lives:
    - from the hand of every beast,
    - from the hand of man, and
    - from the hand of every man's brother.

- I will account for the life of man.

- [6] Whosoever sheds a man's blood, man will shed his blood because GOD [ELOHIM] made man in HIS OWN image [see Genesis 1:26].

- [7] Now
    - be fruitful,
    - multiply,
    - bring forth abundantly in the earth, and
    - multiply therein."

GOD'S Covenant with Noah

[8] GOD (ELOHIM) said to **Noah** and his sons,

- [9] "I establish MY covenant with
    - you,
    - your seed [descendants],
    - [10] every living creature that is with you,
    - every fowl,
    - every cattle,
    - every beast of the earth with you and
    - from all that goes out of the ark to every beast of the earth.

- [11] I will establish MY covenant with you.
    - Never will all flesh be cut off anymore by the waters of a flood.
    - Never will there be a flood anymore to destroy the earth.

- [12] This is the token of the covenant that I made between
    - ME,
    - you, and
    - every living creature that is with you
    - for perpetual generations.

- [13] I set MY bow [rainbow in the cloud].

- MY rainbow will be a token [sign] of the covenant between ME and the earth.

- [14] And it will come to pass, when I bring a cloud over the earth, the rainbow will be seen in the cloud.

- [15] I will remember MY covenant, which is between
    - ME,
    - you, and
    - every living creature of all flesh.

- The waters will never again become a flood to destroy all flesh.

- [16] The rainbow will be in the cloud, and I will look at it to remember the everlasting covenant between GOD [ELOHIM] and every living creature of all flesh on the earth.

49

- [17] The rainbow is the token of the covenant I have established between ME and all flesh upon the earth."

Noah Curses Canaan

[18] The following sons of Noah came out of the ark:
- Shem,
- Ham, and
- Japheth.

Ham was the father of Canaan.

[19] These were the three sons of Noah; from them, the whole earth was populated.

[20] Noah began to farm his land.

He planted a vineyard.

[21] One day, Noah drank wine and became drunk.

Noah was naked in his tent.

[22] Ham, the father of Canaan, saw his father's nakedness and told his brothers Shem and Japheth outside the tent.

[23] Shem and Japheth took a garment and laid it upon their shoulders.

They entered Noah's tent backward and covered the nakedness of their father.

Their faces were turned away from Noah so they didn't see their father's nakedness.

[24] Noah awoke from his drunkenness and knew what his younger son (Ham) had done to him.

[25] Noah said,

- "Cursed be Canaan [son of Ham].

- A servant of servants he will be to his brothers.

50

- ²⁶ Blessed be the LORD GOD [YAHWEH ELOHIM] of Shem.

- Canaan will be Shem's servant.

- ²⁷ GOD [ELOHIM] will enlarge Japheth.

- Japheth will live in the tents of Shem.

- And Canaan will be Japheth's servant."

²⁸ Noah lived three hundred and fifty years after the flood.

²⁹ Noah died when he was nine hundred and fifty years old.

Chapter 11
2100 BC

Tower of Babel

[1] The whole earth was of one language and of one speech.

[2] And it came to pass, as they journeyed from the east, that they found an open area in the land of Shinar (the land of Babylonia) and lived there.

[3] The people said to one another,

- "Let us make bricks and burn them thoroughly."

And they had brick for stone and slime for mortar.

[4] The people said,

- "Let us build a city and a tower whose top may reach heaven.

- Let us make a name for ourselves to ensure we are not scattered abroad upon the face of the whole earth."

[5] The LORD (YAHWEH) came down to see the city and the tower, which the children of men had built.

[6] The LORD (YAHWEH) said,

- "Behold, the people are one, and they all speak one language, and this is what they begin to do?

- Now, nothing they imagine will be too difficult to accomplish.

- [7] Come, let US go down and confuse their language, so they may not understand each other's speech."

[8] So the LORD (YAHWEH) scattered them abroad upon the face of the earth, and they stopped building the city.

[9] Therefore, the city was named Babel because there the LORD (YAHWEH) confused the language of the earth.

From there, the LORD (YAHWEH) scattered the people abroad across the face of the earth.

Generations from Shem to Abram (Abraham)

[10] These are the generations of Shem.

Shem Dies at 600 Years Old

Two years after the flood , when Shem was one hundred years old, he had a son named Arphaxad.

Shem lived five hundred years after Arphaxad was born.

Shem also had other sons and daughters.

Arphaxad Dies at 438 Years Old

[12] Arphaxad was thirty-five years old when he had a son named Salah.

[13] Arphaxad lived four hundred and three years after Salah was born.

Arphaxad also had other sons and daughters.

Salah Dies at 433 Years Old

[14] Salah was thirty years old when he had a son named Eber.

[15] Salah lived four hundred and three years after Eber was born.

Salah also had other sons and daughters.

Eber Dies at 464 Years Old

[16] Eber was thirty-four years old when he had a son named Peleg.

[17] Eber lived four hundred and thirty years after Peleg was born.

Eber also had other sons and daughters.

Peleg Dies at 239 Years Old

[18] **Peleg** was thirty years old when he had a son named **Reu**.

[19] **Peleg** lived two hundred and nine years after **Reu** was born

Peleg also had other sons and daughters.

Reu Dies at 239 Years Old

[20] **Reu** was thirty-two years old when he had a son named **Serug**.

[21] **Reu** lived two hundred and seven years after **Serug** was born.

Reu also had other sons and daughters.

Serug Dies at 230 Years Old

[22] **Serug** was thirty years old when he had a son named **Nahor**.

[23] **Serug** lived two hundred years after **Nahor** was born.

Serug also had other sons and daughters.

Nahor Dies at 148 Years Old

[24] **Nahor** was twenty-nine years old when he had a son named **Terah**.

[25] **Nahor** lived one hundred and nineteen years after **Terah** was born.

Nahor also had other sons and daughters.

Abram (**Abraham**) is Born

[26] **Terah** was seventy years old when he became the father of the following sons:
- **Abram** (GOD renames **Abram** to **Abraham** in Genesis 17:5),
- Nahor[2], and
- Haran.

Terah's Sons

[27] These are the generations of **Terah**.

Terah had the following three sons:

- **Abram**,
- Nahor[2], and
- Haran.

Generations of Tarah

Haran had a son named
- Lot.

[28] Haran died before his father **Terah** in the land of his nativity, Ur of the Chaldees.

[29] **Abram** and his brother Nahor[2] married wives.

The name of **Abram's** wife was
- **Sarai** (GOD renamed **Sarai** to **Sarah** in Genesis 17:15).

The name of Nahor[2]'s wife was
- Milcah.

Milcah was the daughter of
- Haran.

Haran was also the father of
- Iscah.

[30] **Sarai** was barren and had no children.

Terah Dies at 205 Years Old

[31] **Terah** took his son, **Abram**, his nephew Lot (Haran's son), and his daughter-in-law **Sarai** (**Abram's** wife) from the Ur of the Chaldees to the land of Canaan.

When they arrived in Haran City, they settled there.

[32] **Terah** died in Haran City at the age of two hundred and five.

Chapter 12
2091 BC

Abram (Abraham) Travels from Haran to Egypt

[1] The LORD (YAHWEH) said to Abram,

- "Leave your country, relatives, and father's house.

- Go to the land that I will show you.

- [2] I will make you a great nation.

- I will bless you.

- I will make your name great.

- You will be a blessing.

- [3] I will bless those who bless you.

- I will curse him who curses you.

- In you will all families of the earth be blessed."

[4] So Abram departed as the LORD (YAHWEH) had told him.

Lot went with Abram.

Abram was seventy-five years old when he departed the city of Haran.

[5] Abram took with him
- his wife Sarai,
- his nephew Lot,
- all their possessions, and
- the souls (people) whom they had acquired in Haran City.

They traveled to the land of Canaan, and into the land of Canaan, they arrived.

⁶ **Abram** passed through the land of Canaan to the plain of Moreh, which was in Sichem.

And the Canaanites were in the land.

⁷ The LORD (YAHWEH) appeared to **Abram** and said,

- "I will give this land to your seed [descendants]."

There, **Abram** built an altar to the LORD (YAHWEH), WHO had appeared to him.

Abram (Abraham) Travels from Moreh to Bethel

⁸ **Abram** left the plain of Moreh, went to the mountain east of Bethel, and pitched his tent.

Bethel was on the west, and Hai (also spelled Ai) was on the east.

There, **Abram** built an altar to the LORD (YAHWEH) and called upon the name of the LORD (YAHWEH).

⁹ **Abram** continued traveling south.

¹⁰ Since famine was so great in the land, **Abram** went down to Egypt to stay.

¹¹ When **Abram** and **Sarai** were close to entering Egypt, **Abram** said to **Sarai** his wife,

- "I know you are a beautiful woman to look at.

- ¹² Therefore, it shall come to pass, when the Egyptians see you, they will say,

  o 'This is his wife,' and kill me.

- They will kill me, but they will save your life.

- ¹³ Therefore, please tell the Egyptians you are my sister.

- Then they will not kill me, and my soul will live because of you."

Abram (Abraham) Arrives in Egypt

[14] And it came to pass when Abram entered Egypt, the Egyptians saw how beautiful Sarai was.

[15] Pharaoh's princes also saw her and commended her before Pharaoh.

Then Sarai was taken to Pharaoh's house.

[16] Because of Sarai, Pharaoh treated Abram very well, giving Abram
- sheep,
- oxen,
- male and female donkeys,
- male and female servants, and
- camels.

GOD Plagues Pharaoh

[17] But the LORD (YAHWEH) plagued Pharaoh and his house with great plagues because he had taken Sarai, Abram's wife.

[18] Pharaoh called for Abram and said,

- "What have you done to me?

- Why didn't you tell me that Sarai was your wife?

- [19] Why did you say,

  o 'She is my sister ?'

- So I would take her as my wife?

- Now, therefore, take your wife and go on your way."

[20] Pharaoh commanded his men to escort Abram and Sarai away with their belongings.

Chapter 13
2085 BC

Abram (Abraham) Leaves Egypt

[1] Abram departed Egypt and traveled south with
- Sarai,
- Lot, and
- their belongings.

[2] Abram was very rich in
- cattle,
- silver, and
- gold.

[3] Abram continued his journey from the south to a place between Bethel and Hai, which was the same place where he had initially pitched his tent (see Genesis 12:8).

[4] He went to the place of the altar which he had first built.

There, Abram called on the name of the LORD (YAHWEH).

[5] Lot, who also traveled with Abram, had
- flocks,
- herds, and
- tents.

[6] However, the land could not support both Abram and Lot because their flocks and herds required an enormous amount of food.

The land could not sustain them because their substance was so great.

Therefore, they could not remain together.

[7] There was also strife between Abram's herdsmen of his cattle and the herdsmen of Lot's cattle.

The Canaanites and the Perizzites lived in the same land at the time.

[8] Abram said to Lot,

- "Let there be no strife between me and you and my herdsmen and your herdsmen, for we are brothers.

- ^{9} The whole land is before you.

- Please separate yourself from me.

- If you depart to the left, I will go to the right.

- If you depart to the right, I will go to the left."

^{10} Lot looked up and saw all the plain of Jordan.

Lot noticed it was well-watered everywhere, just like the garden of the LORD (YAHWEH), like the land of Egypt as you go to Zoar.

This occurred before the LORD (YAHWEH) destroyed Sodom and Gomorrah.

^{11} Lot chose all the plain of Jordan for himself.

Lot traveled east, and they separated themselves, one from another.

^{12} **Abram** lived in the land of Canaan, and Lot lived in the cities of the plain.

Lot pitched his tent toward the city of Sodom.

^{13} But the men of Sodom were extremely wicked and sinners before the LORD (YAHWEH).

^{14} After Lot separated himself from **Abram**, the LORD (YAHWEH) said to **Abram**,

- "From where you are standing, look
  - northward,
  - southward,
  - eastward, and
  - westward.

- ^{15} I will give you and your seed [descendants] all the land you see, forever.

60

- [16] I will make your seed [descendants] plentiful as the dust of the earth.

- If a man can number the dust of the earth, then your seed [descendants] will also be numbered.

- [17] Arise, walk through the land, in the length of it and in the breadth of it.

- I will give it to you."

[18] Then **Abram** disassembled his tent, traveled to and lived in the plain of Mamre, which is in Hebron.

There **Abram** built an altar to the LORD (YAHWEH).

Chapter 15
2081 BC

The WORD Came to Abram

[1] After these things occurred, the WORD of the LORD (YAHWEH) came to Abram in a vision, saying,

- "Fear not, **Abram**.

- I AM your shield.

- I AM your exceedingly great reward."

[2] **Abram** said to the LORD GOD (YAHWEH ADONAI),

- "LORD GOD [YAHWEH ADONAI], what will YOU give me, seeing that I am childless?

- The only person to inherit my house is Eliezer of Damascus.

- [3] YOU have given me no seed [descendants].

- Therefore, my only heir is a servant who was born in my house."

[4] The WORD of the LORD (YAHWEH) came to **Abram** saying,

- "Your servant, Eliezer of Damascus, will not be your heir.

- But he that will come forth out of your own bowels will be your heir."

[5] The LORD (YAHWEH) took **Abram** outside and said,

- "Look toward heaven.

- Count the stars if you are able to number them; so will your seed [descendants] be numbered."

[6] **Abram** believed in the LORD (YAHWEH) and credited the LORD'S (YAHWEH'S) approval of him because of his righteousness.

7 The LORD (YAHWEH) said to **Abram**,

- "I AM the LORD [YAHWEH] that brought you out of Ur of the Chaldees to give you this land to inherit it."

8 **Abram** said to the LORD GOD (YAHWEH ADONAI),

- "LORD GOD [YAHWEH ADONAI],

- How will I know that I have inherited the land?"

9 The LORD (YAHWEH) said to **Abram**,

- "Bring ME the following,
    o a three-year-old heifer,
    o a three-year-old female goat,
    o a three-year-old ram,
    o a turtledove, and
    o a young pigeon."

10 **Abram** brought the LORD (YAHWEH) all of these and cut them in half; then he laid each piece one against another.

But he did not cut the birds into two separate pieces.

11 When the vultures came down upon the carcasses, **Abram** drove them away.

12 Then when the sun was going down, a deep sleep fell upon **Abram**, and a horror of great darkness fell upon him.

13 The LORD (YAHWEH) said to **Abram**,

- "Know for sure that your seed [descendants] will live as strangers in a land that is not theirs and will serve them.

- They will afflict your descendants for four hundred years.

- 14 And also, I will judge the nation [Egypt] whom they will serve.

- Afterward, your descendants will come out of that nation [Egypt] with great substance.

- [15] As for you, you will go to your fathers [will die] in peace and be buried at a good old age.

- [16] But, in the fourth generation, your descendants will return here again.

- For the sin of the Amorites is not yet full."

[17] And it came to pass that when the sun went down, and it was dark, a smoking furnace and a burning lamp passed between the pieces of animal halves.

Covenant Regarding Land

[18] On the same day, the LORD (YAHWEH) made a covenant with **Abram**, saying,

- "I have given your seed [descendants] this land, from the river of Egypt to the great Euphrates River, the land which is now occupied by the following tribes/clans:
    o [19] Kenites,
    o Kenizzites,
    o Kadmonites,
    o [20] Hittites,
    o Perizzites,
    o Rephaims,
    o [21] Amorites,
    o Canaanites,
    o Girgashites, and
    o Jebusites."

Chapter 17
2067 BC

Covenant—Father of Multiple Nations

¹ When **Abram** was ninety-nine years old, the LORD (YAHWEH) said to him,

- "I AM GOD ALMIGHTY [EL-SHADDAI].

- Walk before ME and be perfect.

- ² I will make MY covenant between ME and you.

- I will multiply you exceedingly."

GOD Changes **Abram's** Name to **Abram** (**Abraham**)

³ **Abram** fell on his face.

GOD (ELOHIM) said to **Abram**,

- ⁴ "As for ME, behold, MY covenant is with you.

- You will be a father of many nations.

- ⁵ Your name will no longer be called **Abram**, but your name will now be called **Abraham**.

- I have made you a father of many nations.

- ⁶ I will make you exceeding fruitful.

- I will make nations from you.

- Kings will come out of you.

- ⁷ I will establish MY covenant between ME and you and your seed [descendants] as an everlasting covenant.

- I will be a GOD [ELOHIM] to you.

- And I will be a GOD [ELOHIM] to your seed [descendants] after you.

- [8] I will give to you and your seed [descendants] after you, the land wherein you are a stranger, all the land of Canaan, for an everlasting possession.

- And I will be their GOD [ELOHIM]."

Circumcised versus Uncircumcised

[9] GOD (ELOHIM) said to Abraham,

- "You and your seed [descendants] must keep MY covenant.

- [10] This is MY covenant, which you must keep, between ME, you, and your seed [descendants] after you:

  - Every male child among you must be circumcised.

  - [11] You must circumcise the flesh of your foreskin.

- The circumcision will be a token of the covenant between ME and you.

- [12] All males must be circumcised when they are eight days old.

- Every male in your generation must be circumcised, including
  - he that is born in the house;
  - he that is bought with money of any stranger, which is not of your seed;
  - [13] he that is born in your house; and
  - he that is bought with your money.

- MY covenant must be in your flesh for an everlasting covenant.

- [14] The uncircumcised male child whose flesh of his foreskin is not circumcised, that soul must be cut off from his people. He has broken MY covenant."

GOD Changes Sarai's (Sarah's) Name to Sarah

¹⁵ GOD (ELOHIM) said to **Abraham**,

- "As for your wife **Sarai**, you must not call her **Sarai**, but **Sarah** will be her name.

- ¹⁶ I will bless **Sarah** and give you a son by her.

- Yes, I will bless **Sarah**, and she will be a mother of nations; kings of people will be among her descendants."

¹⁷ Then **Abraham** fell upon his face and laughed.

Abraham said in his heart,

- "Will a child be born to a one-hundred-year-old man?

- And will **Sarah**, who is ninety years old, have children?"

¹⁸ **Abraham** said to GOD (ELOHIM),

- "Can Ishmael live with your blessing?"

¹⁹ GOD (ELOHIM) said to **Abraham**,

- "**Sarah**, your wife will indeed have your son.

- You will call him **Isaac**.

- I will establish MY covenant with **Isaac** and **Isaac's** seed [descendants] as an everlasting covenant.

- ²⁰ As for Ishmael, I have heard your request.

- I have blessed Ishmael.

- I will make Ishmael fruitful.

- I will multiply Ishmael exceedingly.

- Twelve princes will come from Ishmael's descendants.

- I will make Ishmael a great nation.

- ²¹ But I will establish MY covenant with **Isaac**, to whom **Sarah** will give birth at this set time next year."

²² When GOD (ELOHIM) finished talking with **Abraham**, GOD (ELOHIM) went up from **Abraham**.

²³ As GOD (ELOHIM) had told him, **Abraham** had the flesh of the following people circumcised on the same day:
- Ishmael, **Abraham's** son;
- all the males born in his house;
- all the males bought with his money; and
- every male among the men of **Abraham's** house.

²⁴ **Abraham** was ninety-nine years old when he was circumcised in the flesh of his foreskin.

²⁵ Ishmael, **Abraham's** son, was thirteen years old when he was circumcised in the flesh of his foreskin.

²⁶ **Abraham** and Ishmael were circumcised on the same day.

²⁷ And all of the men of **Abraham's** house, whether born in the house or bought with a stranger's money, were circumcised with **Abraham**.

Chapter 18
2067 BC

GOD Appears to Abraham

¹ The LORD (YAHWEH) appeared to Abraham in the plains of Mamre.

Abraham was sitting at his tent door in the heat of the day.

² Abraham looked up and saw three MEN (YAHWEH and HIS angels) standing nearby.

Abraham ran to meet them from the tent door and bowed toward the ground.

³ Abraham said to the three MEN,

- "My LORD [ADONAI], please don't pass by if I have found favor in your sight.

- ⁴ Let us retrieve some water and wash YOUR feet.

- Please rest YOURSELVES under the tree.

- ⁵ I will retrieve a morsel of bread so you can comfort YOUR hearts.

- After that, YOU can continue on YOUR way."

The three MEN (YAHWEH and HIS angels) said to Abraham,

- "Very well, WE will do as you have said."

⁶ Abraham quickly entered the tent and said to Sarah,

- Quick, make two gallons of fine meal, knead it, and make cakes upon the hearth."

⁷ Abraham ran to the herd and retrieved a good and tender calf.

He gave the calf to his servant, who quickly prepared it.

⁸ **Abraham** took butter, milk, the calf he had dressed, and set it before the three MEN.

Then **Abraham** stood by them under the tree as they ate.

⁹ The three MEN (YAHWEH and HIS angels) said to **Abraham**,

- "Where is **Sarah,** your wife?"

Abraham said to the three MEN,

- "She is in the tent."

¹⁰ The LORD (YAHWEH) said to **Abraham**,

- "I will certainly return to you according to the time of life.
- At that time, your wife **Sarah** will have a son."

Sarah heard the conversation from the tent door, which was behind HIM.

¹¹ Now **Abraham** and **Sarah** were old and well stricken in age.

Sarah had passed the age of childbearing.

¹² Therefore, **Sarah** laughed within herself and said,

- "How can I have the pleasure of childbirth since I am so old, as well as my husband also being old?"

¹³ The LORD (YAHWEH) said to **Abraham**,

- "Why did **Sarah** laugh?
- Why did she question her ability to have a child because of her age?
- ¹⁴ Is anything too hard for the LORD [YAHWEH]?
- At the appointed time, I will return to you, according to the time of life, and **Sarah** will have a son."

¹⁵ Then because Sarah was afraid, she said,

- "I did not laugh."

But the LORD (YAHWEH) said to Sarah,

- "No, but you did laugh."

¹⁶ Then the MEN (YAHWEH and HIS angels) stood up and looked toward the city of Sodom.

Abraham started walking with them to see them on their way.

Sodom and Gomorrah

¹⁷ The LORD (YAHWEH) said to the other two men,

- "Should I hide from Abraham the thing I will do,¹⁸ seeing that Abraham will surely become a great and mighty nation, and all the nations of the earth will be blessed in him? [See Genesis 12:2–3.]

- ¹⁹ For I know him, that he will command his children and his household after him, and they will keep the way of the LORD [YAHWEH], to do justice and judgment.

- The LORD [YAHWEH] may bring upon Abraham that which HE has spoken of him."

²⁰ Then the LORD (YAHWEH) said to Abraham,

- "Because the cry of Sodom and Gomorrah is great and their sin is very grievous, ²¹ I will go down now and see if they have done it according to the cries that have come to ME.

- If not, I will know."

²² The two other men (messengers of YAHWEH) turned their faces away from Abraham and the LORD (YAHWEH) and started traveling toward Sodom.

Abraham stood next to the LORD (YAHWEH).

²³ Abraham drew near and said to the LORD (YAHWEH).

- Will YOU also destroy the righteous with the wicked?

- ²⁴ What if fifty righteous people are within the city?

- Will YOU destroy and not spare the city for fifty righteous people?

- ²⁵ May it be far from YOU to do things like that to kill the righteous with the wicked so that the righteous should be like the wicked.

- May that be far from YOU.

- Shouldn't the JUDGE of all the earth do right?

²⁶ The LORD (YAHWEH) said Abraham,

- "If I find in Sodom fifty righteous people within the city, then I will spare the entire place for their sakes."

²⁷ Abraham said to the LORD (YAHWEH),

- "I have taken it upon myself to speak to the LORD [YAHWEH], but I am but dust and ashes.

- ²⁸ What if forty-five righteous people are in the city?

- Will YOU destroy the city for the lack of five righteous people?"

The LORD (YAHWEH) said to Abraham,

- "If I find forty-five righteous people in the city, I will not destroy it."

²⁹ Abraham spoke again and said to the LORD (YAHWEH),

- "What if forty righteous people are found in the city?"

The LORD (YAHWEH) said to Abraham,

- "I will not destroy the city for the sake of forty righteous people."

[30] **Abraham** said to the LORD (YAHWEH),

- "Oh, LORD [YAHWEH], please don't be angry if I speak again.

- What if thirty righteous people are found in the city?"

The LORD (YAHWEH) said to **Abraham**,

- "I will not destroy the city for the sake of thirty righteous people."

[31] **Abraham** said to the LORD (YAHWEH),

- "I have taken it upon myself to speak to the LORD [YAHWEH].

- What if twenty righteous people are found in the city?"

The LORD (YAHWEH) said to **Abraham**,

- "I will not destroy the city for the sake of twenty righteous people."

[32] **Abraham** said to the LORD (YAHWEH),

- "Oh, LORD [YAHWEH], please don't be angry,

- I will only speak this one last time.

- What if ten righteous people are found in the city?"

The LORD (YAHWEH) said to **Abraham**,

- "I will not destroy the city for the sake of ten righteous people."

[33] When the LORD (YAHWEH) finished HIS conversation with **Abraham**, HE went on HIS way.

Abraham returned to his tent.

Chapter 19
2067 BC

Two Angels Arrive in Sodom

¹ In the evening, the two angels of the LORD (messengers of YAHWEH) arrived at Sodom.

Lot was sitting at the gate of Sodom.

When Lot saw the two angels of the LORD (messengers of YAHWEH), he stood up and met them.

He bowed with his face toward the ground.

² Lot said to the two angels of the LORD (messengers of YAHWEH),

- "Behold, my lords, please turn here and enter your servant's house.

- Stay here for the night and wash your feet.

- Rise up early tomorrow morning and then go on your way."

The two angels of the LORD (messengers of YAHWEH) said to Lot,

- "No, we will sleep in the street tonight."

³ Lot pressured them greatly, and then they turned to Lot and entered his house.

Lot made them a feast, baked them unleavened bread, and they ate.

⁴ But before they lay down, the men of the city, even the men of Sodom, surrounded Lot's house, both old and young men and all the people from every quarter.

⁵ The men of Sodom said to Lot,

- "Where are the men who entered your house tonight?

- Bring them outside to us so that we may have sex with them."

⁶ And Lot went out of his house door to talk with them, and he shut the door behind him.

⁷ Lot said to the men of Sodom,

- "Please, my brethren, do not be so wicked.

- ⁸ Listen, I have two virgin daughters.

- Please, let me bring them to you and do what is good in your eyes.

- But to these men do nothing, for they came under the shadow of my roof."

⁹ The men of Sodom said to Lot,

- "Stand back!

- This fellow [Lot] came to our town to live, and now he thinks he is a judge.

- We will deal worse with you [Lot] than with them."

The men of Sodom pressed hard against Lot and tried to break the door.

¹⁰ But the men (messengers of YAHWEH) put forth their hand, pulled Lot into the house with them, and then shut the door.

¹¹ Then the men (messengers of YAHWEH) struck the men of Sodom at the door with blindness, both small and great, so the men of Sodom exhausted themselves trying to find the door.

¹² The men (messengers of YAHWEH) said to Lot,

- "Do you have anyone else here besides you, such as
  ○ your sons-in-law,
  ○ your sons,
  ○ your daughters, or
  ○ whatsoever you have in this city?

- Take them out of this place.

- [13] We will destroy this place because their cry has become increasingly great before the LORD [YAHWEH].

- The LORD [YAHWEH] has sent us to destroy it."

[14] And Lot went out and spoke to his sons-in-law, who married his daughters.

Lot said to his sons-in-law,

- "Get up and get out of this place!

- For the LORD [YAHWEH] will destroy this city!"

But they interpreted his statements as mocking or teasing them.

[15] When the morning came, the two angels of the LORD (messengers of YAHWEH) rushed Lot, saying,

- "Get up!

- Take your wife and your two daughters, who are here, or else you will be consumed in the iniquity of the city."

[16] And while Lot lingered, the men (messengers of YAHWEH) grabbed his hand, the hand of his wife, and the hand of Lot's two daughters.

The LORD (YAHWEH) was being merciful to Lot.

The angels of the LORD (messengers of YAHWEH) took Lot and set him outside the city.

[17] And it came to pass, once the angels of the LORD (messengers of YAHWEH) brought Lot and his family outside the city, the LORD (YAHWEH) said to Lot,

- "Escape for your life.

- Do not look behind you.

76

- Do not stay anywhere in the plain.

- Escape to the mountain.

- Or else you will be consumed."

[18] Lot said to them (YAHWEH and HIS messengers),

- "Oh, not so, my LORD [ADONAI].

- [19] Behold now, your servant has found grace in YOUR sight, and YOU have magnified YOUR mercy, which YOU have shown to me in saving my life.

- However, I cannot escape to the mountain, or else evil will take me, and I will die.

- [20] Behold now, this city [city of Zoar] is near to flee to, and it is a little one.

- Oh, let me escape there, and my soul will live."

[21] The LORD (ADONAI) said to Lot,

- "See, I have accepted you concerning this request.

- I will not overthrow this city [city of Zoar], for which you have spoken.

- [22] Now hurry and escape there.

- For I cannot do anything until you arrive there."

Therefore, the city's name was Zoar (Zoar means a place of refuge).

[23] The sun had risen upon the earth when Lot entered Zoar.

[24] Then the LORD (YAHWEH) rained out of heaven upon Sodom and Gomorrah brimstone and fire.

[25] And HE overthrew those cities:

- all the plain,
- all the inhabitants of the cities, and
- that which grew upon the ground.

²⁶ But Lot's wife looked back from behind him, and she became a pillar of salt.

Abraham Witnesses Sodom and Gomorrah's Destruction

²⁷ Abraham got up early in the morning to the place where he had stood before with the LORD (YAHWEH).

²⁸ Abraham looked toward Sodom, Gomorrah, and all the land of the plain and saw the country's smoke going up like a furnace.

²⁹ And it came to pass when GOD (ELOHIM) destroyed the cities of the plain (Sodom and Gomorrah), GOD (ELOHIM) remembered Abraham. HE sent Lot out from the middle of the overthrow before HE destroyed the cities in which Lot lived.

Lot Goes to Zoar

³⁰ Lot went to Zoar, where he and his two daughters lived in the mountains.

Lot was afraid to live in Zoar, so he and his two daughters lived in a cave in the mountains.

Moabites and Ammonites

³¹ Lot's firstborn daughter said to Lot's younger daughter,

- "Our father [Lot] is old, and there is not a man on earth to have sex with us.

- ³² Let us make our father drink wine, and we will lie with him.

- That way, we will preserve our father's seed [descendants]."

³³ And they made their father (Lot) drink wine that night.

Lot's firstborn daughter went in and lay down with her father.

Lot was unaware when she had laid down with him and when she arose.

³⁴ And it came to pass on the next day that Lot's firstborn daughter said to her younger sister,

- "Behold, last night I lay with my father.

- Let us also make him drink wine tonight so you can go in and lie with him.

- In this way, we can preserve our father's seed."

³⁵ And they also made their father drink wine that night.

The younger daughter arose and lay down with him.

Lot was unaware when she had lay down next to him or when she arose.

³⁶ Thus both of Lot's daughters became pregnant with their father's child.

Moabites

³⁷ Lot's firstborn daughter gave birth to a son

She called his name
- Moab.

Moab became the father of the Moabites to this day.

Ammonites

³⁸ Lot's younger daughter gave birth to a son.

She called his name
- Benammi.

Benammi became the father of the children of Ammon (Ammonites) to this day.

Chapter 20
2067 BC

Abraham Travels from Mamre to Gerar

¹ Abraham traveled from the plains of Mamre toward the south country, stopping between Kadesh and Shur and living in the town of Gerar.

² Abraham said to the people of Gerar,

- "Sarah is my sister."

Then Abimelech, the king of Gerar, sent for Sarah and took her for himself.

³ GOD (ELOHIM) came to King Abimelech in a dream one night and said to him,

- "Behold, you are a dead man because the woman you took for yourself is already married to a man."

⁴ But Abimelech had not yet come near Sarah and said to GOD (ELOHIM),

- "LORD [ADONAI], will YOU destroy a righteous nation?

- ⁵ Didn't Abraham say to me,

    o 'She is my sister.'

- And Sarah, even Sarah herself, said,

    o 'He is my brother.'

- In the integrity of my heart and innocence of my hands have I done this."

⁶ GOD (ELOHIM) said Abimelech in a dream,

- "Yes, I know that you did this in the integrity of your heart.

- I also withheld you from sinning against ME; therefore, I did not allow you to touch her.

- ⁷ Now return **Sarah** to her husband.

- For **Abraham** is a prophet; he will pray for you, and you will live.

- If you don't restore **Sarah**, know that you will surely die, you and all who are yours."

⁸ Therefore, Abimelech rose early the next morning, called his servants, and told them everything that had happened.

And the men were terrified.

⁹ Then Abimelech called **Abraham** and said to him,

- "What have you done to us?

- What have I done to you to cause you to bring such a great sin on me and my kingdom?

- You have done things to me that should not have been done!

- ¹⁰ What did you see that caused you to do this?"

¹¹ **Abraham** said to Abimelech,

- "Because I thought, surely the fear of GOD [ELOHIM] is not in this place.

- They will kill me for my wife's sake.

- ¹² Yet, indeed, **Sarah** is my sister.

- **Sarah** is the daughter of my father, but not the daughter of my mother.

- And she became my wife.

- ¹³ And it came to pass when GOD [ELOHIM] caused me to leave

81

my father's house. I said to her,

- o This is the kindness you will show me.

- o At every place we go, say,

  - ▪ 'He is my brother.'"

¹⁴ Then Abimelech gave to **Abraham**
- sheep,
- oxen,
- male servants, and
- female servants.

Abimelech also returned **Sarah** to **Abraham**.

¹⁵ Abimelech said to **Abraham**,

- "Behold, my land is before you.

- Live wherever it pleases you."

¹⁶ Abimelech said to **Sarah**,

- "I have given your brother **Abraham** one thousand pieces of silver.

- He is to you a covering of the eyes to all who are with you and all others."

Thus, **Sarah** was vindicated.

¹⁷ **Abraham** prayed to GOD (ELOHIM), and GOD (ELOHIM) healed Abimelech, his wife, and his female servants so they could have children.

¹⁸ For the LORD (YAHWEH) had closed all the wombs of the house of Abimelech because of **Sarah**, **Abraham's** wife.

Chapter 21
2066 BC–2057 BC

Isaac is Born

¹ The LORD (YAHWEH) visited Sarah as HE had said (see Genesis 18:10), and the LORD (YAHWEH) did to Sarah as HE had spoken.

² Sarah conceived and gave birth to a son for Abraham in his old age, at the exact time that GOD (ELOHIM) had spoken to him (see Genesis 17:16).

³ Abraham called the name of his son, who was born to him, whom Sarah had given birth to
- Isaac.

⁴ Abraham circumcised his son Isaac when Isaac was eight days old, as GOD (ELOHIM) had commanded him (see Genesis 17:9–14, 17:23–27).

⁵ Abraham was one hundred years old when his son Isaac was born to him.

⁶ Sarah said to herself,

- "GOD [ELOHIM] has made me laugh so that all who hear about this will laugh with me.

- ⁷ Who would have ever told Abraham that Sarah could have nursed children?

- For I have given birth to a son for Abraham in his old age."

⁸ And the child grew and was weaned.

Abraham made a great feast the same day that Isaac was weaned.

⁹ Sarah saw Ishmael, the son of Hagar the Egyptian who had given birth to him for Abraham, mocking her.

¹⁰ Then Sarah said to Abraham,

- "Cast out this female servant [Hagar] and her son [Ishmael]!

- For the son of this servant [Ishmael] will not be heir with my son, even with **Isaac**."

[11] And the thing was very grievous in **Abraham's** sight because Ishmael was also his son.

[12] Then GOD (ELOHIM) said to **Abraham**,

- "Let it not be grievous in your sight because of Ishmael and because of your woman servant [Hagar].

- In all that **Sarah** has said to you, listen to her voice.

- For in **Isaac** will your seed [descendants] be called.

- [13] I will make a nation of your son Ishmael of the female servant Hagar because Ishmael is also your seed."

[14] So **Abraham** woke up early in the morning, took bread and a bottle of water, and gave them to Hagar.

He put them and her child Ishmael on her shoulder and sent her away.

Hagar departed **Abraham** and wandered in the wilderness of Beersheba (also spelled Beer-Sheba, meaning well of oath).

[15] When the water in the bottle was used up, Hagar put Ishmael under one of the shrubs.

[16] Then Hagar went and sat down facing him a good way off, about a bow shot away (approximately one hundred yards away).

Hagar said to herself,

- "Let me not see the death of the child."

Then Hagar sat over against Ishmael, lifted her voice, and wept.

[17] GOD (ELOHIM) heard the voice of Ishmael.

The angel of GOD (messenger of ELOHIM) called to Hagar from out of heaven, saying,

- "What ails you, Hagar?

- Fear not, for GOD [ELOHIM] has heard the voice of Ishmael where he is.

- ¹⁸ Stand up, pick up Ishmael, and hold him in your hand.

- For I will make him a great nation" (see Genesis 16:10).

¹⁹ Then GOD (ELOHIM) opened her eyes, and she saw a well of water.

She filled the bottle with water and gave Ishmael a drink.

²⁰ GOD (ELOHIM) was with Ishmael as he grew and lived in the wilderness.

Ishmael became an archer.

²¹ Ishmael lived in the wilderness of Paran.

Hagar gave Ishmael a wife who was from the land of Egypt.

²² And it came to pass at that time that Abimelech and Phichol, Abimelech's chief captain, spoke to Abraham, saying,

- "GOD [ELOHIM] is with you in all that you do.

- ²³ Now, therefore, swear to me here by GOD [ELOHIM] that you will not deal falsely with
  - me,
  - nor with my son, and
  - nor with my grandsons.

- But according to the kindness I have done to you, you will do to me and the land where you have stayed."

²⁴ Abraham said to Abimelech and Phichol,

- "I will swear."

²⁵ Then Abraham criticized Abimelech because of a well of water that

Abimelech's servants had violently taken away.

²⁶ Abimelech said to **Abraham**,

- "I know nothing about who has done this thing.

- Neither did you tell me.

- Neither have I ever heard about it.

- Today is the first time I have heard about it."

²⁷ **Abraham** took sheep and oxen and gave them to Abimelech, and both of them made a covenant.

²⁸ **Abraham** also placed seven female lambs from his flock off by themselves.

²⁹ Abimelech said to **Abraham**,

- "Why did you set these seven female lambs off by themselves?"

³⁰ **Abraham** said to Abimelech,

- "These seven female lambs you will take from my hand so that they may be a witness to me that I dug this well."

³¹ Therefore, **Abraham** called the place Beersheba because they both swore an oath there.

³² After **Abraham** and Abimelech made a covenant at Beersheba, Abimelech and Phichol, the chief captain of his host, rose up and returned to the land of the Philistines.

³³ **Abraham** planted a grove of tamarisk trees in Beersheba and called there in the name of the LORD (YAHWEH), GOD EVERLASTING (EL OLAM).

³⁴ **Abraham** stayed in the Philistines' land for many days.

Chapter 22
2054 BC

GOD Tests Abraham

[1] And it came to pass after these things, that GOD (ELOHIM) tested Abraham, saying,

- "Abraham."

Abraham said to GOD (ELOHIM),

- "Here I am."

[2] GOD (ELOHIM) said to Abraham,

- "Now take your son, your only son, Isaac, whom you love, and go to the land of Moriah.

- Offer him there as a burnt offering upon one of the mountains, which I will tell you."

[3] Abraham rose up early in the morning and
- saddled his donkey,
- took two of his young men with him,
- took his son Isaac, and
- took split wood for the burnt offering.

Then they went to the place that GOD (ELOHIM) had told them.

[4] On the third day, Abraham looked up and saw the place in the distance.

[5] Abraham said to the two young men,

- "Wait here with the donkey.

- I and the lad [Isaac] will go over there and worship and then return."

[6] Abraham took the wood for the burnt offering and laid it upon Isaac,

his son.

Abraham also took the fire and the knife in his hand.

Then they both started on their way together.

⁷ Isaac said to Abraham, his father,

- "My father."

Abraham said to Isaac,

- "Here am I, my son."

Isaac said to Abraham,

- "We have the fire and the wood, but where is the lamb for a burnt offering?"

⁸ Abraham said to Isaac,

- "My son, GOD [ELOHIM] will provide HIMSELF a lamb for a burnt offering."

So together, they both continued on their way.

⁹ They arrived at the place that GOD (ELOHIM) told Abraham to go.

Abraham built an altar there and laid the wood in order.

Abraham bound his son Isaac and laid him on the altar upon the wood.

¹⁰ Abraham stretched forth his hand and took the knife to slay Isaac.

¹¹ Then the angel of the LORD (messenger of YAHWEH) called Abraham out of heaven, saying,

- "Abraham, Abraham."

Abraham said to the angel of the LORD (messenger of YAHWEH),

- "Here I am."

¹² The angel of the LORD (messenger of YAHWEH) said to **Abraham**,

- "Do not lay your hand on **Isaac**, nor do anything to him.

- For now, I know that you fear GOD [ELOHIM], seeing you have not withheld your only son from me."

¹³ **Abraham** looked up and saw behind him a ram caught in a thicket by its horns.

Abraham took the ram and offered it as a burnt offering instead of his son **Isaac**.

¹⁴ Then **Abraham** called the name of that place Jehovahjireh (also spelled JEHOVAH-Jireh, meaning the LORD will provide).

And it is still said today,

- "In the mountain of the LORD [YAHWEH], it will be seen."

¹⁵ The angel of the LORD (messenger of YAHWEH) called **Abraham** from out of heaven a second time, saying,

- "The LORD [YAHWEH] says:

  o ¹⁶ 'Because you have done this thing and have not withheld your only son, **Isaac**.

  o I have sworn to MYSELF.

  o ¹⁷ In blessing, I will bless you.

  o In multiplying, I will multiply your seed [descendants]:
    - as numerous as the stars of heaven and
    - as numerous as the sand which is upon the seashore.

  o Your seed [descendants] will possess control of his enemies.

  o In your seed will all nations of the earth be blessed because you have obeyed MY voice.'"

[19] So **Abraham** returned to his two young men, and they stood up and traveled together back to Beersheba, where **Abraham** remained.

Children of Nahor[2] and Milcah

[20] And it came to pass after these things occurred that someone said to **Abraham**,

- "Milcah, your brother Nahor[2]'s wife, has given birth to the following children:
  - [21] Huz [the firstborn son],
  - Buz,
  - Kemuel [the father of Aram],
  - [22] Chesed,
  - Hazo,
  - Pildash,
  - Jidlaph, and
  - Bethuel"—[23] Bethuel became the father of **Rebekah**.

These were the eight sons that Milcah gave birth to for Nahor[2], **Abraham's** brother.

Children of Nahor[2] and Reumah

[24] Nahor[2]'s concubine, whose name was Reumah, gave birth to the following children:
- Tebah,
- Gaham,
- Thahash, and
- Maachah.

Chapter 24
2026 BC

Rebekah

¹ **Abraham** was old and well-stricken in age.

The LORD (YAHWEH) had blessed **Abraham** in all things.

² **Abraham** said to the oldest servant of his house, who ruled over all that **Abraham** had,

- "Please, put your hand under my thigh.

- ³ I will make you swear by the LORD [YAHWEH], the GOD [ELOHIM] of the earth, that you will not take a wife to my son from the daughters of the Canaanites, among whom I live.

- ⁴ But you will go to my country, to my relatives, and take a wife from there for my son **Isaac**."

⁵ The servant said to **Abraham**,

- "What if the woman is unwilling to follow me to this land?

- Must I take your son again to the land you came from?"

⁶ **Abraham** said to his servant,

- "Beware, do not take my son there again.

- ⁷ The LORD GOD [YAHWEH ELOHIM] of heaven, WHO took me from my father's house, and the land of my relatives and WHO spoke to me and WHO swore to me, said,

  - 'I will give this land to your seed [descendants].'

- HE will send HIS angel before you, and you will take a wife for my son from there.

- ⁸ If the woman is unwilling to follow you, you will be clear from

91

this oath with me.

- Only, you will not take my son there again."

[9] The servant put his hand under the thigh of his master **Abraham** and swore to him concerning that matter.

[10] The servant took ten of **Abraham's** camels and departed; all the goods of his master were in his hand.

The servant arose and went to Mesopotamia, to the city of Nahor.

[11] In the evening, the servant stopped by a well of water outside the city and made his camels kneel down.

This was during the same time in the evening that the women in the area went down to the well to draw water.

[12] The servant prayed to the LORD GOD (YAHWEH ELOHIM), saying,

- "O LORD GOD [YAHWEH ELOHIM] of my master **Abraham**.

- Send me good speed [success] on this day and show kindness to my master **Abraham**.

- [13] Behold, I stand here by the well of water as the daughters of the men of the city are coming out to draw water.

- [14] Let it come to pass that the young lady walks by, to whom I will say,

  o 'Please, put down your pitcher so that I may drink.'

- And she will say to me,

  o 'Drink and I will also give your camels water.'

- Let the same woman be the same one YOU have appointed for YOUR servant **Isaac**.

- Thereby, I will know that YOU have shown kindness to my master **Abraham**."

[15] And it came to pass before he had finished speaking that Rebekah, who was born to Bethuel, son of Milcah, the wife of Nahor[2], Abraham's brother, came out with her pitcher on her shoulder.

[16] Rebekah was very beautiful to look at and a virgin; neither had any man had sex with her.

Rebekah went down to the well, filled her pitcher, and came back up.

[17] The servant ran to meet Rebekah and said,

- "Please let me drink a little water from your pitcher."

[18] Rebekah said to the servant,

- "Drink, my lord."

Rebekah quickly lowered her pitcher upon her hand and gave him a drink.

[19] And when she was done giving him a drink, Rebekah said to the servant,

- "I will draw water for your camels also until they have finished drinking."

[20] Rebekah quickly emptied her pitcher into the watering trough and ran again to the well to draw water.

She drew water for all of his camels.

[21] The servant watched Rebekah as he held his peace and wondered whether the LORD (YAHWEH) had made his journey prosperous.

[22] And it came to pass, as the camels finished drinking, the servant took a golden earring weighing two ounces and two gold bracelets for her hands weighing four ounces.

[23] The servant said to Rebekah,

- "Whose daughter are you?

- Please tell me.

- Is there room in your father's house for us to lodge in?"

²⁴ Rebekah said to the servant,

- "I am the daughter of Bethuel, the son of Milcah, whose father was Nahor[2].

- ²⁵ We have enough straw and feed for your camels and room to lodge in."

²⁶ The servant bowed his head and worshipped the LORD (YAHWEH).

²⁷ The servant prayed to LORD GOD (YAHWEH ELOHIM),

- "Blessed be the LORD GOD [YAHWEH ELOHIM] of my master Abraham, WHO has not deprived my master of HIS mercy and truth.

- I, being in the way, the LORD [YAHWEH] led me to the house of my master's brothers."

²⁸ Rebekah ran and told everyone in her mother's house everything that had happened.

Laban—Rebekah's Brother

²⁹ Rebekah had a brother, and his name was Laban. (Laban is listed as a Syrian in Genesis 25:20.)

Laban ran out to the servant at the well.

³⁰ And it came to pass when Laban saw the earring and bracelets upon Rebekah's hands, and when he heard the words of Rebekah explaining what the man had said to her, Laban went to the man who stood by the camels at the well.

³¹ Laban said to the servant,

- "Come in, you who are blessed by the LORD [YAHWEH].

- Why are you standing outside?

- I have prepared the house for you and a room for the camels."

32 The servant went into the house with Laban, then he
- unloaded his camels,
- gave straw and food to the camels, and
- gave water to wash his feet and the feet of the men who were with him.

33 And meat to eat was set before the servant, but he said to Laban,

- "I will not eat until I have explained to you my errand."

Laban said to the servant,

- "Speak on."

34 The servant said to Rebekah's family,

- "I am Abraham's servant.

- 35 The LORD [YAHWEH] has blessed my master greatly, and he has become great.

- The LORD [YAHWEH] has given him flocks, herds, silver, gold, male and female servants, camels, and donkeys.

- 36 Sarah, my master's wife, gave birth to my master Isaac when she was old.

- And to Isaac, Abraham has given all that he has.

- 37 My master Abraham made me swear by saying,

  o 'You will not take a wife to my son Isaac from the daughters of the Canaanites, in whose land I live.

  o 38 But you will go to my father's house and my relatives and find a wife for my son.'

- 39 I said to my master Abraham, saying,

  o 'What if the woman will not follow me back?'

95

- [40] My master **Abraham** said to me,

  - 'The LORD [YAHWEH], before whom I walk, will send HIS angel [messenger of YAHWEH] with you, and prosper your way.

  - And you will take a wife for my son **Isaac**, from among my relatives and of my father's house.

  - [41] Then you will be clear from my oath.

  - But when you come to my relatives and if they do not give you a wife for my son, then you will be clear from my oath.'

- [42] And I came this day to the well and said,

  - 'O LORD GOD [YAHWEH ELOHIM] of my master **Abraham**, now prosper the way in which I go.

  - [43] Behold, I stand by the well of water.'

  - And it shall come to pass that when the virgin comes forth to draw water, and I say to her,

    - 'Please give me a little water from your pitcher to drink.'

  - [44] She will say to me,

    - 'Drink, and I will also give your camels water.'

  - Let the same be the woman whom the LORD [YAHWEH] has appointed for my master's son **Isaac**.

- [45] And before I finished speaking in my heart, behold, **Rebekah** came forth with her pitcher on her shoulder, and she went down to the well and drew water.

- I said to her,

  - 'Please give me a drink of water.'

- ⁴⁶ And she quickly put down her pitcher of water from her shoulder and said to me,

    - o 'Drink, and I will also give your camels water.'

- So I drank, and she also made the camel drink.

- ⁴⁷ Then I asked her,

    - o 'Whose daughter are you?'

- And Rebekah said to me,

    - o 'I am the daughter of Bethuel, Nahor [2]'s son, to whom Milcah gave birth.'

- Then I put the earrings upon her face and the bracelets upon her hands.

- ⁴⁸ And I bowed down my head and worshipped the LORD [YAHWEH] and blessed the LORD GOD [YAHWEH ELOHIM] of my master Abraham, WHO had led me in the right way to take my master's niece to his son Isaac.

- ⁴⁹ And now, if you will deal kindly and truly with my master, tell me if she can return with me.

- And if you will not allow her to return with me, please tell me so I will know what to do next."

⁵⁰ Then Laban and Bethuel said to the servant,

- "This has obviously come from the LORD [YAHWEH]: we cannot say anything to you, bad or good.

- ⁵¹ Rebekah is before you, take her and go, and let her be your master's son's wife, as the LORD [YAHWEH] has spoken."

⁵² And it came to pass that when Abraham's servant heard their words, he worshipped the LORD (YAHWEH), bowing himself to the earth.

⁵³ And the servant brought forth jewels of silver and gold and clothing and gave them to Rebekah.

He also gave Rebekah's brother Laban and her mother (no name) precious things.

⁵⁴ Then they ate and drank; he and the men who came with him stayed all night.

The next morning, they got up and said,

- "Send me away to my master."

⁵⁵ Laban and Rebekah's mother said,

- "Let Rebekah stay with us a few days, at least ten days.

- After that, she can go with you."

⁵⁶ The servant said to them,

- "Don't hinder me, since the LORD [YAHWEH] has prospered my way.

- Send me away so I may go to my master."

⁵⁷ Laban and Rebekah's mother said to the servant,

- "We will call Rebekah and ask her what she wants to do."

⁵⁸ Laban and the family called Rebekah and said to her,

- "Will you go with this man?"

Rebekah replied,

- "I will go."

⁵⁹ Rebekah and her nurse went with Abraham's servant and the servant's men.

⁶⁰ Laban and his family blessed Rebekah, saying,

- "You are our sister.

- Be the mother of thousands of millions.

- Let your seed [descendants] conquer all who hate them."

⁶¹ Rebekah and her nurse rode upon the camels and followed the servant.

The servant took Rebekah and went away.

Isaac **Meets** Rebekah

⁶² Isaac returned from the well called Lahairoi (also spelled Lahai-Roi); for he lived in the south country.

⁶³ Isaac went out to meditate in the field in the evening.

He looked up and saw that the camels were coming.

⁶⁴ Rebekah looked up, and when she saw Isaac, she dismounted the camel.

⁶⁵ Rebekah said to the servant,

- "What man is this walking in the field to meet us?"

The servant said to Rebekah,

- "It is my master."

Therefore, Rebekah took her veil and covered herself.

⁶⁶ The servant told Isaac everything he had done.

⁶⁷ Then Isaac took Rebekah into his mother Sarah's tent.

Isaac had intercourse with Rebekah, she became his wife, and he loved her.

Isaac was comforted after his mother's death.

Chapter 25
2006 BC–1978 BC

Generations of Abraham, Isaac, and Jacob

[1] Then Abraham took another wife, and her name was Keturah.

[2] Keturah gave birth to the following sons:
- Zimran,
- Jokshan,
- Medan,
- Midian,
- Ishbak, and
- Shuah.

[3] Jokshan became the father of the following sons:
- Sheba[3] and
- Dedan[2].

Dedan[2] became the father of the following sons:
- Asshurim,
- Letushim, and
- Leummim.

[4] Midian became the father of the following sons:
- Ephah,
- Epher,
- Hanoch,
- Abidah, and
- Eldaah.

All these were the children of Keturah, Abraham's wife.

[5] Abraham gave all that he had to Isaac.

[6] But Abraham gave gifts to his sons born from his concubines and sent them away eastward from Isaac, his son, to the east country.

Abraham Dies at 175 Years Old

[7] **Abraham** lived to be one hundred and seventy-five years old.

[8] Then **Abraham** gave up the ghost and died at a good old age, an old man, full of years, and was gathered by his ancestors.

[9] **Abraham's** sons **Isaac** and Ishmael buried him in the cave of Machpelah, in the field of Ephron, the son of Zohar the Hittite, which is before Mamre.

[10] This was the field that **Abraham** purchased from the sons of Heth. **Abraham** and **Sarah**, his wife, were buried there.

[11] After Abraham's death, GOD (ELOHIM) blessed his son **Isaac**; **Isaac** lived by the well called Lahairoi (also spelled Lahai-Roi).

Ishmael's Sons

[12] These are the generations of Ishmael, **Abraham's** son, whom Hagar the Egyptian, **Sarah's** handmaid, gave birth to for **Abraham**.

[13] The following are the names of the twelve sons of Ishmael, by their names and according to their generations:
- Nebajoth (firstborn son),
- Kedar,
- Adbeel,
- Mibsam,
- [14] Mishma,
- Dumah,
- Massa,
- [15] Hadar,
- Tema,
- Jetur,
- Naphish, and
- Kedemah.

[16] These were the sons of Ishmael:
- their names,
- their towns,
- their castles, and
- the twelve princes, according to their nations.

Ishmael Dies at 137 Years Old

[17] Ishmael lived for one hundred and thirty-seven years.

Then he gave up the ghost and died and was gathered by his people.

[18] And they lived from Havilah to Shur, located before Egypt, as you go toward Assyria.

Ishmael died in the presence of all his brethren.

Esau and Jacob are Born

[19] These are the generations of Isaac, Abraham's son.

Abraham became the father of
- Isaac.

[20] Isaac was forty years old when he married Rebekah, the daughter of Bethuel, the Syrian of Padanaram (also spelled Padan-Aram), and the sister of Laban the Syrian.

[21] Isaac prayed to the LORD (YAHWEH) for his wife because she could not have children.

The LORD (YAHWEH) answered Isaac's prayer, and Rebekah, his wife, conceived.

[22] But the children struggled together within her.

Rebekah said to herself,

- "If it is so, why am I experiencing this?"

Rebekah went and asked the LORD (YAHWEH).

[23] The LORD (YAHWEH) said to Rebekah,

- "Two nations are in your womb.

- Two types of people will be separated from your bowels.

- The one people will be stronger than the other people.

102

- The older will serve the younger."

²⁴ When **Rebekah** gave birth, behold, there were twins in her womb.

²⁵ The first came out red all over like a hairy garment.

They named him
- Esau.

²⁶ After that came his brother.

His hand took hold of Esau's heel.

They named him
- **Jacob**.

Isaac was sixty years old when **Rebekah** gave birth to Esau and **Jacob**.

²⁷ The boys grew.
- Esau was a cunning hunter, a man of the field, and
- **Jacob** was a plain man living in tents.

²⁸ **Isaac** loved Esau because he enjoyed eating Esau's venison.

However, **Rebekah** loved **Jacob**.

Esau Sells His Firstborn Rights

²⁹ One day, **Jacob** was boiling stew.

Esau came in from the field and was faint.

³⁰ Esau said to **Jacob**,

- "Please feed me with some of that red stew, for I am faint."

Therefore, Esau was also called Edom (Edom means red).

³¹ **Jacob** said to Esau,

- "Sell me your birthright today."

103

[superscript]32[/superscript] Esau said to **Jacob**,

- "I am at the point of dying.

- What profit will this birthright do for me?"

[superscript]33[/superscript] **Jacob** said to Esau,

- "Swear to me this day."

And Esau swore to **Jacob** and sold his birthright to **Jacob**.

[superscript]34[/superscript] Then **Jacob** gave Esau bread and lentil stew.

Esau ate and drank, stood up, and went on his way.

Thus, Esau despised his birthright.

Chapter 26
1977 BC

Isaac and King Abimelech

¹ In addition to the first famine that occurred during Abraham's time, there was another famine in the land.

Isaac, Abraham's son, went to Abimelech, king of the Philistines, in Gerar.

² The LORD (YAHWEH) appeared to Isaac and said,

- "Do not go down to Egypt.

- Sojourn in this land, and I will be with you and bless you.

- For unto you and your seed [descendants], I will give all these countries.

- I will perform the oath I swore to your father Abraham.

- ⁴ I will make your seed [descendants] multiply as the stars of heaven.

- I will give your seed [descendants] all these countries.

- In your seed [descendants will all the nations of the earth be blessed ⁵ because Abraham
  - obeyed MY voice;
  - kept MY charge;
  - kept MY commandments;
  - kept MY statutes; and
  - kept MY laws."

Isaac Claims Rebekah is His Sister

⁶ And Isaac remained in Gerar.

⁷ The men of Gerar asked Isaac about his wife Rebekah.

Isaac said to the men of Gerar,

- "She is my sister" (Abraham also said this about Sarah in Genesis 20:2).

Isaac was afraid to say,

- "She is my wife" because he thought the men of Gerar would kill him for Rebekah because she was so beautiful to look at.

[8] And it came to pass when Isaac had lived in Gerar for a long time that Abimelech, the king of the Philistines, looked out of a window and saw Isaac and Rebekah, his wife, being affectionate with one another.

[9] Abimelech called Isaac and said,

- "Surely, she is your wife.

- How sad that you said:

  - 'She is my sister?'"

Isaac said to Abimelech,

- "I said it because I thought I would be killed for her."

[10] Abimelech said to Isaac,

- "What is this you have done to us?

- One of the people of Gerar might have lain down with your wife, and you would have brought guilt upon us."

[11] King Abimelech said to all his people,

- "Anyone who touches this man or his wife will be put to death."

Water Rights

[12] Isaac planted crops in the land and received a hundred times what he planted in the same year.

The LORD (YAHWEH) blessed him.

106

¹³ Isaac became great and went forward and grew until he was very great; ¹⁴ he had
- flocks,
- herds, and
- a great store of servants.

The Philistines envied him.

¹⁵ Therefore, all the wells his father's servants had dug in the days of Abraham his father, the Philistines had stopped them and filled them with earth.

¹⁶ Abimelech said to Isaac,

- "Go away from us, for you are much mightier than we are."

¹⁷ Isaac departed from there, pitched his tent in the valley of Gerar, and lived there.

¹⁸ Isaac dug again the wells of water, which had been dug in the days of Abraham, his father.

For the Philistines had stopped them after the death of Abraham.

Isaac called the names of the wells by the same names his father had called them.

Isaac's **First Well**

¹⁹ Isaac's servants dug a well in the valley of Gerar and found a spring there.

²⁰ The herdsmen of Gerar had disagreements with Isaac's herdsmen, saying,

- "The water is ours."

So Isaac called the well Esek (Esek means quarrel) because the herdsmen quarreled with him there.

Isaac's **Second Well**

²¹ Then **Isaac's** herdsmen dug another well and had disagreements over that one also.

So **Isaac** called the name of that well Sitnah (Sitnah means hostility).

Isaac's **Third Well**

²² **Isaac** and his men left that place and dug another well.

There the herdsmen did not argue about the well, so **Isaac** named the well Rehoboth (Rehoboth means open spaces).

Isaac said to himself,

- "Now the LORD [YAHWEH] has made room for us, and we shall be fruitful in the land."

GOD Appears to **Isaac** in Beersheba

²³ **Isaac** left the valley of Gerar and went to Beersheba.

²⁴ The LORD (YAHWEH) appeared to **Isaac** the same night.

The LORD (YAHWEH) said to **Isaac**,

- "I AM the GOD [ELOHIM] of **Abraham** your father.

- Fear not, for I AM with you.

- I will bless you.

- I will multiply your seed [descendants] for MY servant **Abraham's** sake."

²⁵ **Isaac** built an altar there in Beersheba and called upon the name of the LORD (YAHWEH).

There, **Isaac** pitched his tent, and his servants dug a well.

²⁶ Then Abimelech went to **Isaac** from Gerar with Ahuzzath, a friend of King Abimelech, and Phichol, the chief captain of King Abimelech's army.

²⁷ Isaac said to them,

- "Why did you come and see me since you hate me and were the ones who sent me away?"

²⁸ They said to Isaac,

- "We saw for certain that the LORD [YAHWEH] was with you, and we said to ourselves,
    - 'Let there now be an oath between us, even between us and you.'

- So let us make a covenant with you.

- ²⁹ You will do us no harm as we have not touched you.

- And as we have done unto you nothing but good and have sent you away in peace.

- You are now the blessed of the LORD [YAHWEH]."

³⁰ Isaac made them a feast, and they ate and drank.

³¹ They woke up early in the morning and swore to one another.

Isaac sent them away, and they departed from him in peace.

³² It came to pass the same day that Isaac's servants came and gave him an update regarding the well they had dug.

Isaac's servants said to him,

- "We have found water."

³³ And Isaac named the well Shebah (Shebah means oath).

Therefore, the city's name is Beersheba (also spelled Beer-Sheba) to this day.

Esau Marries Two Women

³⁴ At forty years old, Esau married two women :
109

- Judith, the daughter of Beeri the Hittite and
- Bashemath, the daughter of Elon the Hittite.

[Note: The same Bashemath listed in Genesis 26:34 is listed as Adah[2] in Genesis 36:2. Therefore, this person will be listed as Adah[2]/Bashemath in future text.]

[35] Isaac and Rebekah were emotionally distressed because Esau married two Hittite women.

Chapter 28
1928 BC

Isaac Blesses Jacob

[1] Isaac called Jacob, blessed him, and charged him, saying,

- "You shall not take a wife from the daughters of Canaan.

- [2] Go to Padanaram [also spelled Padan-Aram] to the house of Bethuel, your mother's father, and take a wife from the daughters of Laban, your mother's brother.

- [3] May GOD ALMIGHTY [EL-SHADDAI]
    o bless you,
    o make you fruitful, and
    o multiply you
    o so that you may be a multitude of people.

- [4] And may GOD ALMIGHTY [EL-SHADDAI] give you and your seed [descendants] the blessing of Abraham.

- May you inherit the land wherein you are now a stranger, the land which GOD [ELOHIM] gave to Abraham."

[5] Then Isaac sent Jacob away.

Jacob went to Padanaram to Laban, son of Bethuel the Syrian.

Laban was the brother of Rebekah, Jacob, and Esau's mother.

[6] Esau saw that
- Isaac blessed Jacob;
- Isaac sent Jacob away to Padanaram to take him a wife from there;
- Isaac blessed Jacob;
- Isaac gave Jacob a charge, saying,

    o "You will not take a wife of the daughters of Canaan;" and

- **7** **Jacob** obeyed his father and his mother by going to Padanaram.

8 Esau, seeing that the daughters of Canaan were not pleasing to his father **Isaac**, **9** went to see his uncle Ishmael and married, in addition to the wives he already had

- Mahalath, the daughter of Ishmael, who was **Abraham's** son, and the sister of Nebaioth.

10 **Jacob** left Beersheba and traveled toward Haran.

11 When the sun was setting, **Jacob** stopped at a good resting place, lighted the area, and rested for the night.

Jacob took stones from that place, used them for his pillows, and laid down to sleep.

12 **Jacob** dreamed, and behold, he saw a ladder standing upright on the earth.

The top of the ladder reached heaven.

Jacob saw the angels of GOD (messengers of ELOHIM) ascending and descending on the ladder.

GOD Speaks to Jacob

13 And behold, the LORD (YAHWEH) stood above the ladder and said to **Jacob**,

- "I AM the LORD GOD [YAHWEH ELOHIM] of **Abraham**, your father, and the GOD [ELOHIM] of **Isaac**.

- I will give you and your seed [descendants] the land you are lying on.

- **14** Your seed [descendants] will be as the dust of the earth.

- Your seed [descendants] will spread abroad to the west, east, north, and south.

- In you and in your seed [descendants] will all the families of the earth be blessed.

112

- ¹⁵ And behold, I AM with you.

- I will protect you in all places, wherever you go.

- I will bring you again into this land.

- For I will not leave you until I have done that which I have spoken to you."

¹⁶ **Jacob** awoke from his sleep and said to himself,

- "Surely the LORD [YAHWEH] is in this place, and I did not know it."

¹⁷ **Jacob** became afraid and said to himself,

- "How dreadful [alarming] is this place!

- This place is none other than the house of GOD [ELOHIM], and this is the gate of heaven."

¹⁸ **Jacob** rose early in the morning, took the stones that he had used as pillows, set them up in a pillar, and poured oil on top of them.

¹⁹ **Jacob** called the name of the place Bethel (Bethel means holy place); the name of that city was previously called Luz.

10 Percent Tithe

²⁰ **Jacob** made a vow, saying,

- "If GOD (ELOHIM) will
  - be with me,
  - will protect me in my travels,
  - give me bread to eat, and
  - give me clothes to wear
  - ²¹ so that I can return to my father's house in peace,
  - then the LORD [YAHWEH] will be my GOD [ELOHIM].

- ²² This stone, which I have set up for a pillar, shall be GOD'S [ELOHIM'S] house.

- And of all that YOU shall give me, I will give YOU a tenth [one-tenth of the tithe]."

Chapter 31
1908 BC

Jacob Leaves Laban

¹ Jacob heard the words of Laban's sons, saying,

- "Jacob has taken away all that was our father's, and of that which was our father's, he has received all this glory."

² Jacob noticed that Laban's facial expression and attitude toward him were different than before.

³ The LORD (YAHWEH) said unto Jacob,

- "Return to the land of your fathers and to your relatives.

- I will be with you."

⁴ Jacob sent for Rachel and Leah, who were tending his flock in the field.

⁵ When they arrived, Jacob said to Rachel and Leah,

- "I see your father looks at me differently than before.

- But the GOD [ELOHIM] of my father has been with me.

- ⁶ You know that with all my power, I have served your father.

- ⁷ Your father has deceived me and changed my wages ten times.

- But GOD [ELOHIM] did not allow him to hurt me.

- ⁸ If Laban said,

  o 'The speckled will be your wages,'

- Then all the cattle produced speckled offspring.

- If Laban said,

- o 'The streaked will be your wages,'

- Then all the cattle produced streaked offspring.

- 9 Therefore, GOD [ELOHIM] has taken the cattle of your father and given them to me.

- 10 And it came to pass when the cattle conceived, I lifted my eyes and saw in a dream the rams which leaped upon the cattle were streaked, speckled, and gray-spotted."

- 11 And the angel of GOD [messenger of ELOHIM] said to me in a dream,

  - o 'Jacob.'

- I said to the angel of GOD [messenger of ELOHIM],

  - o 'Here I am.'

- 12 And the angel of GOD [messenger of ELOHIM] said to me,

  - o 'Look up and see all the rams that leap on the cattle, which are streaked, speckled, and gray-spotted.

  - o For I have seen all that Laban does to you.

  - o 13 I am the GOD [EL] of Bethel where you anointed the pillar and where you made a vow to ME. [See Genesis 28:18–22.]

  - o Now rise and leave this land and return to the land of your ancestors.'"

14 Rachel and Leah answered Jacob, saying,

- "There is not any portion or inheritance for us in our father's house?

- 15 Our father Laban counts us as strangers.

- For he has sold us and spent all the money you paid us.

- ¹⁶ All the riches that GOD [ELOHIM] took from our father are rightfully ours and our children's.

- Now whatever GOD [ELOHIM] has said to you, do."

¹⁷ Jacob stood up and set his sons and wives on the camels.

¹⁸ Jacob carried away all his cattle and goods, all of which he had obtained in Padanaram.

He headed toward his father Isaac in the land of Canaan.

¹⁹ Laban was shearing his sheep when Jacob and his family departed.

Unbeknownst to Laban and Jacob, Rachel had stolen her father's household idol and took it with her.

²⁰ Jacob did not tell Laban, the Syrian, that he and his family were leaving.

²¹ So Jacob fled with all that he had.

He passed over the river and traveled toward Mount Gilead.

²² The third day after Jacob departed, someone finally told Laban that Jacob had left.

²³ Then Laban and his relatives pursued Jacob for seven days.

They found and overtook Jacob in the mountains of Gilead.

²⁴ GOD (ELOHIM) came to Laban, the Syrian, in a dream at night.

GOD (ELOHIM) said to Laban,

- "Be careful not to say anything good or bad to Jacob."

²⁵ Then Laban found Jacob.

Jacob pitched his tent in the mountains.

Laban and his relatives pitched their tents in the mountains of Gilead.

26 Laban said to **Jacob**,

- "What have you done?

- You deceived me and took my daughters away like captives taken with the sword.

- 27 Why did you leave secretly and deceive me?

- Why did you steal from me?

- Why did you not tell me you were leaving?

- I would have sent you away with happiness, with songs, with tambourines, and with a harp.

- 28 You did not even allow me to kiss my sons and my daughters?

- Your actions were foolish.

- 29 It is in the power of my hand to hurt you.

- But the GOD [ELOHIM] of your father spoke to me last night, saying,

    o 'Be careful not to say anything good or bad to **Jacob**.'

- 30 I know you want to leave because you yearn for your father's house, but why did you steal my gods?"

31 **Jacob** said to Laban,

- "Because I was afraid.

- I thought you would forcibly take your daughters from me.

- 32 As for your idols, whomever you find with your gods, let him not live.

- In front of my relatives, go and look for anything that belongs to you and take it."

Jacob did not know that Rachel had stolen Laban's idols.

³³ So Laban went into Jacob's tent and Leah's tent.

Then he went into the tents of the two maidservants (Zilpah, Leah's maid, and Bilhah, Rachel's maid), but he did not find his idols.

Then Laban departed Leah's tent and entered Rachel's tent.

³⁴ Rachel had actually taken Laban's images, put them in the camel's saddle, and sat on them.

Laban searched the entire tent but found nothing.

³⁵ Rachel said to her father Laban,

- "Father, let it not displease my lord that I cannot stand up.

- For the custom of women is upon me."

Laban continued searching but did not find the idols.

³⁶ Jacob was angry and said to Laban,

- "What is my trespass?

- What is my sin that you have so hotly pursued after me?

- ³⁷ Now that you have searched through all my stuff, what have you found that is your household stuff?

- Whatever you have found, set it here before our relatives so that they can judge between us both.

- ³⁸ I have been with you for twenty years.

- Your sheep and your female goats have safely given birth to their young, and I have not eaten any of the rams of your flock.

- [39] That which was torn apart by beasts, I did not bring to you. I bore the loss of it.

- I also paid for all lost animals during the day and night, just as you demanded.

- [40] There I was, working during the day while the drought consumed me and the frost consumed me by night, all the while having many sleepless nights.

- [41] I have been in your house for twenty years.

- I served you for fourteen years in order to receive your two daughters and six additional years for your cattle.

- And you have changed my wages ten times.

- [42] Had the GOD [ELOHIM] of my father, the GOD [ELOHIM] of Abraham, and the fear of Isaac, not been with me, you surely would have sent me away empty-handed.

- GOD [ELOHIM] has seen my suffering and the labor of my hands and reprimanded you last night."

[43] Laban answered Jacob and said,

- "These daughters are my daughters, and these children are my children.

- These cattle are my cattle, and all you see is mine.

- However, what can I do today for my daughters or their children to whom they have given birth?

- [44] Therefore, let us make a covenant [treaty], you and I, and let our covenant be a witness between me and you."

[45] Jacob took a stone and stood it up as a pillar.

[46] Jacob said to his relatives,

- "Go and gather stones."

His relatives took stones and stacked them on the ground.

Then they ate a meal together on the heap of stones.

⁴⁷ Laban called the heap of stones Jegarsahadutha (also spelled Jegar-Sahadutha).

But Jacob called it Galeed.

⁴⁸ Laban said to Jacob,

- "This heap of stone is a witness between me and you today."

Therefore, the name of the heap of stone was called Galeed ⁴⁹ and also Mizpah (Mizpah means to watch).

For Laban said to Jacob,

- "May the LORD [YAHWEH] watch between me and you when we are absent one from another.

- ⁵⁰ If you hurt my daughters or if you marry other wives besides my daughters, GOD [ELOHIM] will be watching us even if no one else is around.

- GOD [ELOHIM] is the witness of our covenant.

- ⁵¹ Behold, I have cast this heap of stone and pillar between me and you.

- ⁵² This heap is a witness, and the pillar is a witness that I will not pass over this heap of stones to harm you. And you will not pass over this heap of stones and this pillar to hurt me.

- ⁵³ May the GOD [ELOHIM] of Abraham, the GOD [ELOHIM] of Nahor, and the GOD [ELOHIM] of their father judge between us."

Jacob swore by the fear of his father Isaac.

⁵⁴ Then Jacob offered a sacrifice to GOD (ELOHIM) upon the mountain and called his relatives over to eat bread.

They ate bread and stayed all night in the mountains.

[55] Laban woke up early in the morning, kissed his sons and his daughters, and blessed them.

Then Laban departed and returned to his place.

Chapter 32
1906 BC

Jacob Sends a Message to Esau

¹ Jacob went on his way, and the angels of GOD (messengers of ELOHIM) met him.

² When Jacob saw them, he said,

- "This is GOD'S [ELOHIM'S] camp."

Therefore, he named the place Mahanaim (Mahanaim means two camps).

³ Jacob sent messengers before him to Esau, his brother, into the land of Seir, which was in the country of Edom.

⁴ Jacob said to the messengers,

- "This is what you will say to my lord Esau,

- 'Your servant Jacob says this to you,

  - I have sojourned with Laban and stayed there until now.

  - ⁵ I have
    - oxen,
    - donkeys,
    - flocks,
    - male servants, and
    - female servants.

  - And I have sent messengers to tell my lord that I request that I may find grace in your sight.'"

⁶ The messengers gave the message to Esau and returned.

The messengers said to Jacob,

- "We went to your brother Esau, who came to meet us.

- Four hundred men were with him."

[7] After hearing this, Jacob was greatly afraid and distressed.

He divided the people and animals with him, the flocks, the herds, and the camels, into two groups.

[8] Jacob said to himself,

- "If Esau attacks one group, then the other group will escape."

[9] Jacob prayed to GOD (ELOHIM), saying,

- "O GOD [ELOHIM] of my father Abraham and GOD [ELOHIM] of my father Isaac, the LORD [YAHWEH] WHO said to me,

    o 'Return to your country.

    o Return to your ancestors.

    o And I will deal well with you.'

- [10] I am not worthy of the least of all the mercies and truth YOU have shown YOUR servant.

- For with my staff, I passed over this Jordan River, and now I have become two groups.

- [11] Please, deliver me from the hand of my brother, from the hand of Esau, for I fear him because he will try to kill me along with the mothers and their children.

- [12] YOU said to me,

    o 'I will surely do you good and make your seed [descendants] as numerous as the sand of the sea, which is so numerous they cannot be numbered.'"

[13] So Jacob stayed there that same night.

Jacob took the following drove of animals from his herd as a present for his brother Esau:

124

- [14] two hundred female goats,
- twenty male goats,
- two hundred ewes,
- twenty rams,
- [15] thirty female camels with their colts,
- forty cows,
- twenty female donkeys, and
- ten young donkeys.

[16] **Jacob** delivered the animals into the hands of his servants, each drove by themselves, and said,

- "Pass over before me and put a space between each group of animals."

[17] **Jacob** said to the group of servants leading the first drove,

- "When my brother Esau meets you, he will ask you,

    o 'To whom do you belong?

    o Where are you going?

    o Whose animals are these before you?'

- [18] Then you will say to Esau,

    o 'They belong to your servant **Jacob**.

    o It is a present sent to my lord Esau.

    o And look, **Jacob** is also behind us.'"

[19] **Jacob** commanded the servants who were leading the second, third, and all subsequent droves, saying,

- "In this manner, you will speak to Esau when you find him."

- [20] And say to him moreover,

    o 'Behold, your servant **Jacob** is behind us.'"

Jacob thought to himself,

- "I will appease Esau with my presents before my arrival, then I will look at Esau's face to determine if he will accept me."

²¹ So Esau's present, the drove of animals, departed before Jacob.

Jacob lodged that night in his camp.

²² That night, Jacob woke up and passed over the Jabbok River with his
- two wives (Leah and Rachel),
- two female servants (Zilpah and Bilhah), and
- eleven sons.

²³ Jacob also sent with them everything he had.

Jacob Wrestles with a Man

²⁴ Jacob was left alone.

And there, Jacob wrestled with a man until daybreak.

²⁵ When the man saw that he was not prevailing against Jacob, he touched the socket of Jacob's thigh /hip area, dislocating the joint.

²⁶ The man said to Jacob,

- "Let me go. It is almost daybreak."

Jacob said to the man,

- "I will not let you go unless you bless me."

²⁷ The man said to Jacob,

- "What is your name?"

Jacob said to the man,

- "Jacob."

Jacob's Name Will Be Changed to Israel

²⁸ The man said to **Jacob**,

- "Because you have overcome your struggle with GOD [ELOHIM] and with man, your name will no longer be called **Jacob** but will be called **Israel**" (**Israel** means GOD prevails).

²⁹ **Jacob** said to the man,

- "Please, tell me your name."

The man said to **Jacob**,

- "Why do you want to know my name?"

Then the man blessed **Jacob** there.

³⁰ **Jacob** said to himself,

- "For I have seen GOD [ELOHIM] face-to-face, and my life is preserved."

[Note: **Jacob** states that he saw GOD face-to-face, implying that GOD was the one WHO actually wrestled with him. However, the Bible does not specifically say that GOD was the man WHO wrestled with **Jacob** or spoke to **Jacob**; for example, it does not say, "GOD said." Different translations conflicted on whether this was an angel of GOD or GOD, and Numbers 23:19 tells us that GOD is not human. Therefore, the *SSB* feels it would be disrespectful to imply GOD lost a wrestling match with a human. The *SSB* will only imply that a man in human form wrestled with **Jacob**, and the man's statement in Genesis 32:28 foreshadows GOD'S statement to **Jacob** in Genesis 35:10.]

³¹ As **Jacob** passed over Penuel, the sun rose upon him, and he halted upon his thigh.

³² Therefore, to this day, the children of Israel do not eat the muscle of the thigh/hip socket because the man (GOD) touched the muscle in the socket of **Jacob's** thigh/hip.

Chapter 35
1906 BC

GOD Tells Jacob to Go to Bethel

¹ GOD (ELOHIM) said to Jacob,

- "Arise, go up to Bethel, and live there.

- Make an altar to GOD [EL] WHO appeared to you when you fled from the face of your brother Esau."

² Jacob said to his household and to all that were with him,

- "Put away the strange gods that are among you, be clean, and change your garments.

- ³ Let us go up to Bethel, and there I will make an altar to GOD [EL], WHO answered me in the day of my distress and was with me in the way I went."

⁴ They gave Jacob all the strange gods in their hands and all the earrings in their ears, and Jacob hid them under the oak tree by Shechem City.

⁵ They journeyed, and the terror of GOD (ELOHIM) was upon the cities around them.

Therefore, the people of those cities did not pursue the sons of Jacob.

Eventually, ⁶ Jacob and his household arrived in Luz, also called Bethel, which was in the land of Canaan.

⁷ While there, Jacob built an altar and called the place Elbethel (also spelled EL-Bethel, meaning GOD of the house of GOD) because there, GOD (ELOHIM) appeared to him when he fled from the face of his brother Esau.

⁸ But Deborah, Rebekah's nurse, died and was buried under an oak tree beneath Bethel.

Therefore, it was called Allonbachuth (also spelled Allon-Bachuth, meaning oak of the weeping).

GOD Changes Jacob's Name to Israel

⁹ GOD (ELOHIM) appeared to Jacob again when he came out of Padanaram and blessed him.

¹⁰ GOD (ELOHIM) said to Jacob,

- "Your name is Jacob.

- Your name will not be called Jacob anymore.

- Your name will be Israel."

And GOD (ELOHIM) called his name Israel.

[Note: From this point forward, whenever the person Jacob is mentioned, he will be identified as Israel/Jacob because GOD renamed him Israel. However, whenever the country of Israel is referred to, it will be identified without highlighted text, such as Israel or Jacob.]

¹¹ GOD (ELOHIM) said to Jacob,

- "I AM GOD ALMIGHTY [EL-SHADDAI].

- Be fruitful and multiply.

- A nation and a company of nations will come from you.

- Kings will come from your loins.

- ¹² I will give you and your seed [descendants] after you the land I gave Abraham and Isaac."

¹³ Then GOD (ELOHIM) went up from where HE had talked with Israel/Jacob.

¹⁴ Israel/Jacob set up a stone pillar in the place where GOD (ELOHIM) had talked with him.

Israel/Jacob poured a drink offering and oil on the stone pillar.

129

¹⁵ Israel/Jacob called the name of the place where GOD (ELOHIM) spoke with him Bethel (Bethel means house of GOD).

Benjamin is Born

¹⁶ They journeyed from Bethel.

As they were approaching the city of Ephrath, Rachel started to go into labor.

Rachel's labor pains were very painful.

¹⁷ And it came to pass, when Rachel was in hard labor, the midwife (no name mentioned) said to Rachel,

- "Fear not.

- You will have this son."

¹⁸ It came to pass, as Rachel's soul was departing (as she was dying), that she named the baby
- Benoni.

But his father, Israel/Jacob, named him
- Benjamin.

Rachel Dies

¹⁹ Rachel died and was buried on the way to the city of Ephrath, which is Bethlehem.

²⁰ Israel/Jacob set a stone pillar on Rachel's grave, which is the pillar of Rachel's grave to this day.

²¹ Israel/Jacob continued traveling, spreading his tent beyond the Tower of Edar.

²² And it came to pass, when Israel/Jacob lived in the land, that Reuben went and lay with Bilhah, his father's concubine.

Israel/Jacob heard about it and became angry.

At this time, there were twelve sons of Israel/Jacob.

²³ Leah had the following sons:
- Reuben (Israel/Jacob's firstborn),
- Simeon,
- Levi,
- Judah,
- Issachar, and
- Zebulun.

²⁴ Rachel had the following sons:
- Joseph and
- Benjamin.

²⁵ Bilhah, Rachel's handmaid, had the following sons:
- Dan and
- Naphtali.

²⁶ Zilpah, Leah's handmaid, had the following sons:
- Gad and
- Asher.

These were the sons of Israel/Jacob, who were born to him in Padanaram.

Israel/Jacob Goes to Mamre to See Isaac

²⁷ And Israel/Jacob went to see his father Isaac in Mamre, the city of Arbah, which is Hebron, where Abraham and Isaac resided together.

Isaac Dies at 180 Years Old

²⁸ Isaac died when he was one hundred and eighty years old.

²⁹ Isaac gave up the ghost and died, being gathered by his ancestors.

He was old and full of days.

Isaac's sons Esau and Israel/Jacob buried him.

Chapter 46
1875 BC

Israel/Jacob Travels to Egypt

[1] Israel/Jacob started his journey with all that he had and went to Beersheba, where he offered sacrifices to the GOD (ELOHIM) of his father Isaac.

GOD Appears to Israel/Jacob at Beersheba

[2] GOD (ELOHIM) appeared to Israel/Jacob in a vision at night.

GOD (ELOHIM) said to Israel/Jacob,

- "Jacob, Jacob!"

Israel/Jacob said to GOD (ELOHIM),

- "Here I am."

[3] GOD (ELOHIM) said Israel/Jacob,

- "I AM GOD [EL], the GOD [ELOHIM] of your father.

- Fear not in going down to Egypt.

- I will make a great nation from you while you are there.

- [4] I will go down with you to Egypt. ·

- I will also bring you back up from Egypt again.

- Joseph will put his hand upon your eyes when you die."

[5] Israel/Jacob stood up, and from Beersheba, the sons of Israel carried Jacob, their father, their little ones, and their wives in the wagons that Pharaoh provided.

[6] They took their cattle and their goods, which they had obtained while in the land of Canaan.

132

Israel/Jacob Arrives in Egypt

Then they entered Egypt, Israel/Jacob, and all his seed/family with him:
- [7] his sons,
- his grandsons,
- his daughters,
- his granddaughters, and
- all his seed (children) he brought with him into Egypt.

Israel/Jacob's Children Who Entered Egypt

[8] These are the names of the children of Israel/Jacob and his sons, who entered Egypt, Israel/Jacob and his sons: Reuben, Israel/Jacob's firstborn.

Children of Israel/Jacob and Leah

[9] Reuben was the father of the following sons:
- Hanoch,
- Phallu (also spelled Pallu),
- Hezron, and
- Carmi.

[10] Simeon was the father of the following sons:
- Jemuel (also spelled Nemuel in 1 Chronicles 4:24),
- Jamin,
- Ohad,
- Jachin (also spelled Jarib in 1 Chronicles 4:24),
- Zohar (also spelled Zerah in 1 Chronicles 4:24), and
- Shaul (son of a Canaanite woman).

[11] Levi was the father of the following sons:
- Gershon,
- Kohath, and
- Merari.

[12] Judah was the father of the following sons:
- Er (died in the land of Canaan),
- Onan (died in the land of Canaan),
- Shelah,
- Pharez (also spelled Perez), and

- Zerah.

Pharez was the father of the following sons:
- Hezron[2] and
- Hamul.

¹³ Issachar was the father of the following sons:
- Tola,
- Puvah (also spelled Puah in Numbers 26:23 and 1 Chronicles 7:1),
- Job (also spelled Jashub in Numbers 26:24 and 1 Chronicles 7:1), and
- Shimron.

¹⁴ Zebulun was the father of the following sons:
- Sered,
- Elon[2], and
- Jahleel.

¹⁵ These were Leah and Israel/Jacob's sons, whom they had in Padanaram, in addition to his daughter Dinah.

Israel/Jacob and Leah had a total of thirty-three children.

Children of Israel/Jacob and Zilpah

¹⁶ Gad was the father of the following sons:
- Ziphion (also spelled Zephon in Numbers 26:15),
- Haggi,
- Shuni,
- Ezbon (also spelled Ozni in Numbers 26:16),
- Eri,
- Arodi (also spelled Arod in Numbers 26:17), and
- Areli.

¹⁷ Asher was the father of the following sons:
- Jimnah,
- Ishuah,
- Isui, and
- Beriah.

Asher also had a daughter whose name was Serah.

Beriah was the father of the following sons:
- Heber and
- Malchiel.

[18] These were the sons of Zilpah and Israel/Jacob.

Laban gave Zilpah to his daughter Leah to be her servant.

Israel/Jacob and Zilpah had a total of sixteen children.

Children of Israel/Jacob and Rachel

[19] Rachel and Israel/Jacob had the following sons:
- Joseph and
- Benjamin.

[20] Joseph and Asenath, the daughter of Potiphera, priest of On, in Egypt, had the following sons:
- Manasseh and
- Ephraim.

[21] Benjamin was the father of the following sons:
- Belah,
- Becher,
- Ashbel,
- Gera,
- Naaman,
- Ehi,
- Rosh,
- Muppim,
- Huppim (also spelled Hupham in Numbers 26:39), and
- Ard.

[22] These were the sons of Rachel and Israel/Jacob.

Israel/Jacob and Rachel had a total of fourteen children.

Children of Israel/Jacob and Bilhah

[23] Dan was the father of
- Hushim (also spelled Shuham in Numbers 26:42).

²⁴ Naphtali was the father of the following sons:
- Jahzeel (also spelled Jahziel in 1 Chronicles 7:13),
- Guni,
- Jezer, and
- Shillem (also spelled Shallum in 1 Chronicles 7:13).

²⁵ These were the sons of Bilhah and Israel/Jacob.

Laban gave Bilhah to his daughter Rachel to be her servant.

Israel/Jacob and Bilhah had a total of seven children.

Total Family Taken to Egypt

²⁶ Israel/Jacob took sixty-six souls (family members) to Egypt, which came from his loins.

This number does not include the wives of Israel/Jacob's sons.

²⁷ Joseph had two sons born to him while in Egypt.

Israel/Jacob took seventy souls (family members) to Egypt.

Israel/Jacob Arrives in Goshen

²⁸ Israel/Jacob sent Judah ahead of him to greet Joseph and obtain directions to Goshen.

Then they arrived in the land of Goshen.

²⁹ Joseph prepared his chariot and went to Goshen to meet his father Israel/Jacob.

When Joseph presented himself to his father, he hugged him around his neck and cried on his neck for a long time.

³⁰ Israel/Jacob said unto Joseph,

- "Now let me die since I have seen your face and know that you are alive."

³¹ Joseph said to his brothers and his father's house,

136

- "I will go see Pharaoh and say to him,

  - 'My brothers and my father's house, which were in the land of Canaan, are here with me now.

  - 32 The men are shepherds, and their trade has been cattle feeding.

  - They have brought their flocks, herds, and all they have.'

- 33 Then Pharaoh will call for you and ask,

  - 'What is your occupation?'

- 34 You will say,

  - 'Your servants' trade is raising cattle. We've raised cattle from our youth until now, just like our ancestors.'

- After saying this, Pharaoh will allow you to live in Goshen since shepherds are an abomination to the Egyptians."

Chapter 48
1859 BC

Israel/Jacob Blesses Manasseh and Ephraim

[1] One day, someone said to Joseph,

- "Your father is very sick."

So Joseph went to see Israel/Jacob with his two sons
- Manasseh and
- Ephraim.

[2] When Joseph arrived, someone said to Israel/Jacob,

- "Your son Joseph has come to see you."

Israel/Jacob strengthened himself and sat up on the bed.

[3] Israel/Jacob said to Joseph,

- "GOD ALMIGHTY [EL-SHADDAI] appeared to me at Luz, in the land of Canaan, and blessed me.

- [4] GOD ALMIGHTY [EL-SHADDAI] said to me,

    o 'I will make you fruitful.

    o I will multiply you.

    o I will make of you a multitude of people.

    o I will give this land to you and your seed [descendants] after you as an everlasting possession.'

Israel/Jacob Claims Ephraim and Manasseh as His Sons

- [5] And now regarding your two sons Ephraim and Manasseh, who were born to you in the land of Egypt before I reunited with you in Egypt, are mine.

- They will be mine as Reuben and Simeon are mine.

- [6] And your children, who are born after Ephraim and Manasseh, will be yours and will be called after the name of their brothers in their inheritance.

- [7] As for me, when I came from Padan, Rachel died by my side and along the way to Ephrath City, in the land of Canaan.

- But there was only a little way to go to the city of Ephrath.

- So I buried her there on the way to the city of Ephrath, which is the same as Bethlehem."

[8] Then **Israel/Jacob** noticed Joseph's sons and said,

- "Who are these?"

[9] Joseph said to his father,

- "They are my sons, whom GOD [ELOHIM] has given me in this place."

Israel/Jacob said to Joseph,

- "Please, bring them to me, and I will bless them."

[10] **Israel's/Jacob's** eyes were dim because of old age, so he could not see.

Joseph brought his sons close to **Israel/Jacob**.

Israel/Jacob kissed them and embraced them.

[11] **Israel/Jacob** said to Joseph,

- "I did not think I would ever again see your face, Joseph.

- But now GOD [ELOHIM] has also shown me the faces of your seed [children]."

139

[12] Joseph brought them out from between his knees and bowed with his face to the earth.

[13] Joseph moved his sons closer to Israel/Jacob.

Ephraim (the younger son) was on Joseph's right hand toward Israel/Jacob's left hand.

Manasseh (the older son) was on Joseph's left hand toward Israel/Jacob's right hand.

[14] Israel/Jacob stretched out his right hand and laid it upon Ephraim's head, the youngest son.

Israel/Jacob deliberately laid his left hand upon Manasseh's head, the firstborn son.

[15] Israel/Jacob blessed Joseph by saying,

- "GOD [ELOHIM], before whom my fathers Abraham and Isaac walked.

- The GOD [ELOHIM], WHO fed me all my life to this day.

- [16] The angel [messenger of ELOHIM], who redeemed me from all evil.

- Bless these boys and let my name be named on them and the name of my fathers, Abraham and Isaac.

- Let them multiply greatly throughout the earth."

[17] When Joseph saw that his father had laid his right hand upon the head of Ephraim (the younger son), it displeased him.

So Joseph lifted his father's right hand to remove it from Ephraim's head and placed it on Manasseh's head.

[18] Joseph said to his father,

- "No, my father, Manasseh, is the firstborn.

- Put your right hand upon his head."

140

[19] **Israel/Jacob** refused and said to Joseph,

- "I know my son, I know.

- Manasseh [the older son] will also become a people and will be great.

- But Manasseh's younger brother Ephraim will be greater than he.

- Ephraim's seed [descendants] will become a multitude of nations."

[20] **Israel/Jacob** blessed Ephraim and Manasseh that day, saying,

- "In you, **Israel** will bless its people by saying,

    o 'May GOD [ELOHIM] make you as Ephraim and as Manasseh.'"

In this way, **Israel/Jacob** positioned Ephraim (the younger son) before Manasseh (the older son).

[21] **Israel/Jacob** said to Joseph,

- "Look, I am dying.

- But GOD [ELOHIM] will be with you and bring you again to the land of your fathers.

- [22] Moreover, I have given you one portion of land above your brothers, which I took out of the hand of the Amorite with my sword and bow."

Notes

Index

152

155

156

164

166

172

174

176

180

181

About the Author

Major Bruce Benedict, USA, Retired

Major Bruce Benedict, U.S. Army, Retired, is the owner of The Sunday School Bible, LLC. He spent thirty-nine years in the Department of Defense—serving twenty-one years on active duty and eighteen years in the federal government, defense contracting, and private sector. Throughout his career, he served as a Military Intelligence Officer, Counterintelligence Special Agent, Senior Project Manager, and Senior Program Manager. He has served in Germany, Panama, Japan, Bahrain, Iraq, and Afghanistan.

Bruce is a certified Project Management Professional (PMP) with the Project Management Institute, a certified executive leadership coach through ACT Inc., and a certified John Maxwell leadership coach, speaker, and trainer. As a Senior Program Manager, he served for seven years as the GG-15 Chief of Training for DoD advanced counterintelligence training. While in the private sector, he led the successful development of Verizon's first Cyber Threat Intelligence Platform Service.

He was also the owner of Battlefield Resumes, LLC, which for ten years assisted veterans in finding new careers after military service. He is the author of three Battlefield Resume books: *Operation: Job Search*, *Operation: Civilian Resume*, and *Operation: Federal Resume*.

Bruce is a GOD-fearing Christian who loves GOD and HIS SON, JESUS CHRIST. He is the owner of The Sunday School Bible, LLC, which helps both believers and nonbelievers more easily read, comprehend, and understand the Bible through meticulous formatting. Learn more at TheSundaySchoolBible.com.

www.ingramcontent.com/pod-product-compliance
Lightning Source LLC
Chambersburg PA
CBHW051832090426
42736CB00011B/1761